WORLDWIDE THREATS TO THE HOMELAND

HEARING

BEFORE THE

COMMITTEE ON HOMELAND SECURITY
HOUSE OF REPRESENTATIVES

ONE HUNDRED THIRTEENTH CONGRESS

SECOND SESSION

SEPTEMBER 17, 2014

Serial No. 113–85

Printed for the use of the Committee on Homeland Security

Available via the World Wide Web: http://www.gpo.gov/fdsys/

U.S. GOVERNMENT PUBLISHING OFFICE

93–367 PDF   WASHINGTON : 2015

For sale by the Superintendent of Documents, U.S. Government Publishing Office
Internet: bookstore.gpo.gov Phone: toll free (866) 512–1800; DC area (202) 512–1800
Fax: (202) 512–2104 Mail: Stop IDCC, Washington, DC 20402–0001

COMMITTEE ON HOMELAND SECURITY

MICHAEL T. MCCAUL, Texas, *Chairman*

LAMAR SMITH, Texas
PETER T. KING, New York
MIKE ROGERS, Alabama
PAUL C. BROUN, Georgia
CANDICE S. MILLER, Michigan, *Vice Chair*
PATRICK MEEHAN, Pennsylvania
JEFF DUNCAN, South Carolina
TOM MARINO, Pennsylvania
JASON CHAFFETZ, Utah
STEVEN M. PALAZZO, Mississippi
LOU BARLETTA, Pennsylvania
RICHARD HUDSON, North Carolina
STEVE DAINES, Montana
SUSAN W. BROOKS, Indiana
SCOTT PERRY, Pennsylvania
MARK SANFORD, South Carolina
CURTIS CLAWSON, Florida

BENNIE G. THOMPSON, Mississippi
LORETTA SANCHEZ, California
SHEILA JACKSON LEE, Texas
YVETTE D. CLARKE, New York
BRIAN HIGGINS, New York
CEDRIC L. RICHMOND, Louisiana
WILLIAM R. KEATING, Massachusetts
RON BARBER, Arizona
DONDALD M. PAYNE, JR., New Jersey
BETO O'ROURKE, Texas
FILEMON VELA, Texas
ERIC SWALWELL, California
VACANCY
VACANCY

BRENDAN P. SHIELDS, *Staff Director*
JOAN O'HARA, *Acting Chief Counsel*
MICHAEL S. TWINCHEK, *Chief Clerk*
I. LANIER AVANT, *Minority Staff Director*

(II)

CONTENTS

WORLDWIDE THREATS TO THE HOMELAND

Wednesday, September 17, 2014

U.S. HOUSE OF REPRESENTATIVES,
COMMITTEE ON HOMELAND SECURITY,
Washington, DC.

The committee met, pursuant to call, at 10:08 a.m., in Room 311, Cannon House Office Building, Hon. Michael T. McCaul [Chairman of the committee] presiding.

Present: Representatives McCaul, King, Rogers, Broun, Meehan, Duncan, Chaffetz, Palazzo, Barletta, Daines, Perry, Sanford, Clawson, Thompson, Jackson Lee, Clarke, Higgins, Richmond, Keating, Barber, Payne, O'Rourke, Vela, and Swalwell.

Chairman MCCAUL. The Committee on Homeland Security will come to order.

The committee is meeting today to examine world-wide threats to the security of the homeland of the United States. Before we begin today, I would like to remind our guests that demonstrations from the audience, including the use of signs, placards, T-shirts, as well as verbal outbursts, are a violation of the rules of the House. I would like to thank our guests for their cooperation in maintaining order and decorum during today's hearing.

I now recognize myself for an opening statement.

Secretary Johnson, Director Comey, Director Olsen, we have asked you to come before the committee today to discuss the array of threats facing the U.S. homeland and the Government's response. The chief concern of ours is the proliferation of terrorist safe havens around the world. The 9/11 commission's No. 1 recommendation was to use all elements of National power to deny sanctuary to terrorist groups. Yet we have seen safe havens spread with alarming speed in recent years.

Such territory makes it far easier for terrorist groups to train recruits and hatch plots against the West. During this administration, no less than three extremist sanctuaries have emerged or expanded in Syria, Iraq, and Libya. In Afghanistan, if the administration goes forward with the plan to withdraw our troops like they did in Iraq, we might see terrorists reclaiming the territory from which they planned 9/11.

Our obvious and most immediate concern is the Islamic State of Iraq and Syria, or ISIS. I agree with the President that this group does not represent a legitimate state, but it is, rather, a cabal of butchers peddling a violent and perverted brand of Islam. However, it should never have been taken—taken the beheading of two Americans for our Government—it should never have taken that to wake up the American people to this menace.

We have known for many months that ISIS was surging and represented the top threat to the United States. But the White House dithered without taking action and the President played down the danger. Despite recent U.S. strikes against the group, ISIS still holds onto thousands of square miles of territory where they are able to operate their terrorist army. Recent estimates indicate that they may have up to 30,000 fighters, of which 2,000 or so are Americans and Europeans.

These radicalized Westerners represent an exceptionally grave threat to the U.S. homeland because of their militant training, extremist connections, ease of travel, and intimate knowledge of the West. Today, we expect to hear about the administration's strategy to detect, deter, and disrupt the return of these foreign fighters to the U.S. territory and that of our allies. Let us be clear, our Nation is at war with this group and the twisted ideology it is seeking to spread.

We must consider all instruments of National power to roll back and defeat these fanatics now and destroy them wherever they emerge. For if we do not take the fight to the enemy overseas, we risk having to fight them here at home.

Our military efforts must include airstrikes in Syria to cut off the head of the snake. Top military advisers to the President, including the chairman of the joint chiefs, General Martin Dempsey, have said that to defeat ISIS, its safe haven in Syria must be destroyed. I agree with him. I hope the President is taking the advice of his top commanders and generals in the Pentagon.

But ISIS is not the only threat we face. I hope we hear today how your agencies are working together to address the wider danger from violent Islamist extremism here at home and abroad. The White House has presented a false narrative in recent years about this threat, claiming, for instance, that al-Qaeda was on its heels, on the path to defeat, has been decimated, while in reality, al-Qaeda network has grown and materialized into a deadly global franchise with a spider web of affiliates and ideologically-similar groups attempting to fill the power vacuums across the Middle East, Africa, and Southeast Asia.

The ideological struggle against violent Islamist extremists is taking place not just overseas, but also here at home. There have been more than 70 home-grown violent Jihadist plots or attacks in the United States since 9/11, according to the Congressional Research Service. More than two-thirds of them have been uncovered or have taken place in only the past 5 years.

Many of the suspects were radicalized, at least in part, by on-line Islamist propaganda, including the Boston Marathon bombers and the Fort Hood attacker, a tool ISIS excels at and utilizes.

Additionally, Federal authorities indicted—just yesterday, indicted a U.S. citizen from Rochester for raising money, recruiting, and facilitating training for ISIS.

While the United States continues to battle physical threats posed by terrorist organizations, we must also be vigilant protecting the homeland against asymmetric threats like cyber attacks from state or non-state actors.

President Obama recently noted that the cyber threat is one of the most serious economic and National security challenges we face as a Nation. Sadly, many experts believe the Nation is woefully underprepared to protect itself in this domain. In a recent report from the bipartisan Policy Center, former 9/11 commissioners described the U.S. cyber preparedness as being at pre-September 11 levels.

Last month, Defense Secretary Hagel said the world is exploding all over. I agree with Secretary Hagel's assessment. We look forward to your testimony here today, surveying the threat landscape and elaborating on how we are countering those set against us and our interests.

Before I turn it over to the Ranking Member Thompson, I would like to note that this is the first time that the FBI director has appeared before this committee. Sir, we very much appreciate your presence here today.

If I could ask that the Members be cordial to him so that we will hopefully have his return appearance before this committee.

Additionally, this is likely one of the last Congressional appearances for NCTC Director, Matt Olsen, who has announced his retirement. We thank you for your service, sir, over the years—25 years of service to the Government, Director Olsen, and we appreciate you being here and everything that you have done to protect Americans here in the homeland. It has been a real honor to work with you.

Secretary Johnson, you have been on the job at DHS for 9 months, and I appreciate your good work and outstanding relationship that we have built over those years of—or months that you have taken office. I look forward to having you appear before this committee again.

Thanks for your—if I could just also, I was in New York yesterday. Secretary Johnson was leading the Governors in New York and New Jersey, the FBI, CBP, Homeland Security officials, the Joint Terrorism Task Force in such a professional manner. It was really refreshing to see that kind of leadership coming from our Department on a very serious topic. So, thank you for your leadership, sir.

[The statement of Chairman McCaul follows:]

STATEMENT OF CHAIRMAN MICHAEL T. MCCAUL

SEPTEMBER 17, 2014

Secretary Johnson, Director Comey, and Director Olsen—we've asked you to come before the committee today to discuss the array of threats facing the U.S. homeland and the Government's response.

A chief concern of ours is the proliferation of terrorist safe havens around the world. The 9/11 Commission's No. 1 recommendation was to use "all elements of National power" to deny sanctuary to terrorist groups, yet we have seen safe havens spread with alarming speed in recent years. Such territory makes it far easier for terrorist groups to train recruits and hatch plots against the West.

During this administration, no less than three extremist sanctuaries have emerged or expanded—in Syria, Iraq, and Libya. In Afghanistan, if the administration goes forward with its plan to withdraw our troops like they did in Iraq, we might see terrorists reclaiming the territory from which they planned 9/11.

Our obvious and most immediate concern is the Islamic State of Iraq and Syria, or ISIS. I agree with the President that this group does not represent a legitimate "state" but is rather a cabal of butchers peddling a violent and perverted brand of Islam. However, it should never have taken the beheading of two Americans for our Government to wake up the American people to this menace. We have known for many months that ISIS was surging and represented the top threat to the United

States. But the White House dithered without taking action, and the President played down the danger.

Despite recent U.S. strikes against the group, ISIS still holds onto thousands of square miles of territory where they are able to operate their terrorist army. Recent estimates indicate that they may have up to 30,000 fighters, of which 2,000 or so are Americans and Europeans. These radicalized Westerners represent an exceptionally grave threat to the U.S. homeland because of their militant training, extremist connections, ease of travel, and intimate knowledge of the West.

Today, we expect to hear about the administration's strategy to deter, detect, and disrupt the return of these foreign fighters to U.S. territory and that of our allies.

Let us be clear: Our Nation is at war with this group and the twisted ideology it is seeking to spread. We must consider all instruments of National power to rollback and defeat these fanatics now and destroy them wherever they emerge. Or, if we don't take the fight to the enemy overseas, we risk having to fight them here at home.

Our military efforts must include airstrikes in Syria to cut of the head of the snake. Top military advisors to the President, including the Chairman of the Joint Chiefs General Martin Dempsey, have said that to defeat ISIS its safe haven in Syria must be destroyed. I agree with him, and I hope the President is taking the advice of his top commanders and generals.

But ISIS is not the only threat we face. I hope we hear today how your agencies are working to address the wider danger from Violent Islamist Extremism here at home and abroad.

The White House has presented a false narrative in recent years about this threat, claiming for instance that al-Qaeda was "on its heels," "on the path to defeat," and had been "decimated." While, in reality, the al-Qaeda network has grown and materialized into a deadly global franchise, with a spider web of affiliates and ideologically-similar groups attempting to fill the power vacuums across the Middle East, Africa, and South East Asia.

The ideological struggle against Violent Islamist Extremism is taking place not just overseas, but also here at home. There have been more than 70 home-grown violent jihadist plots or attacks in the United States since 9/11, according to the Congressional Research Service. More than two-thirds of them have been uncovered or have taken place in only the past 5 years. Many of the suspects were radicalized at least in part by on-line Islamist propaganda, including the Boston Marathon bombers and the Fort Hood attackers, a tool ISIS excels at utilizing.

Additionally, last night Federal authorities indicted a U.S. citizen from Rochester, NY for raising money, recruiting, and facilitating travel for ISIS.

While the United States continues to battle "physical threats" posed by terrorist organizations, we must also be vigilant in protecting the homeland against asymmetric threats like cyber attacks from state and non-state actors. President Obama recently noted that the "cyber threat is one of the most serious economic and National security challenges we face as a Nation." Sadly, many experts believe the Nation is woefully underprepared to protect itself in this domain. In a recent report from the Bipartisan Policy Center, former 9/11 Commissioners described the U.S. cyber preparedness as being at pre-September 11 levels.

Last month, Defense Secretary Hagel said "The world is exploding all over." I agree with his assessment and we look forward to your testimony today surveying the threat landscape, and elaborating on how we are countering those set against us and our interests.

Before I turn it over to Ranking Member Thompson, I would note this is the first time the FBI director has appeared before this committee, and we very much appreciate your presence. Additionally, this is likely one of the last Congressional appearances for NCTC Director Matt Olsen who has announced his retirement. We thank you for your service, Director Olsen, and appreciate you being here. It has been a true honor to work with you. Secretary Johnson, you've been on the job at DHS for 9 months. I appreciate our good working relationship and look forward to having you appear before the committee for some time to come.

Chairman MCCAUL. With that, the Chairman now recognizes the Ranking Member, Mr. Thompson.

Mr. THOMPSON. Thank you, Mr. Chairman. I also thank you for holding this very important hearing. However, we are also fortunate to have an exceptionally accomplished and knowledgeable panel of witnesses to discuss the current threat picture.

Secretary Johnson, welcome back. You have offered informative and useful testimony before this committee, and I expect today will be no different.

Direct Comey, it is a great pleasure to have the bureau participate in today's discussion. As the Chairman has said, this is the FBI's maiden voyage before this committee. We look forward to your testimony. I hope that it won't be your last. We will work on that, I am sure.

Mr. Olsen, your years of Federal service, the Chairman has already spoken to, thank you for all the contributions you have made. I am certain the future is still very bright for you. So, thank you very much. I wish you the best in that transition.

Mr. Chairman, 13 years ago this week, just days after the horrific September 11 terrorist attack, then-President George W. Bush addressed Congress and the Nation. In his address, President Bush stated, "Our war on terror begins with al-Qaeda. And it will not end until every terrorist group of global reach has been found, stopped, and defeated."

Thirteen years later, there have been some successes, particularly against core al-Qaeda. But, as we know, not all terrorist groups have been found, stopped, and defeated.

Those of us who were in the audience when President Bush delivered his address could not have predicted how the terrorist threat would evolve. At this time, Congress was completely focused on preventing another large-scale attack on U.S. soil.

In 2001, we understood al-Qaeda to be a centralized organization. No thought was given to the prospect that al-Qaeda would franchise terrorism and inspire satellite groups in the Arabian Peninsula and Africa. The prospect that an attack would be carried out by a lone-wolf actor with no direct training or support from al-Qaeda barely entered the discussion.

We were thinking that terrorist groups were focused on taking human lives. We did not predict that in a decade after September 11, state actors or terrorist groups would try to devastate our economy and steal valuable intellectual property by targeting our cyber infrastructure.

Finally, we could not have imagined that on the eve of the 13th anniversary of 9/11, another American President would come before the American people to make the case for defeating and destroying a terrorist organization. Indeed, the threat from the Islamic State of Iraq and Lebanon is legitimate and warrants attention.

That said, the situation on the ground in Syria is fluid and complex. Defeating and destroying ISIL in this context, is no easy task. I cannot stress enough the need for vigilance and care, particularly should we decide to partner with individuals on the Syria and to try and defeat ISIL.

In addition to our efforts abroad, we need to remain vigilant and improve the preparedness and resilience at home. Last month's arrest of Don Morgan illustrates my long-standing view that we must reject specific ethnic or religious profiles of would-be terrorists. Violent extremism has no race, ethnicity, religion, or culture, and there is no single profile or pathway for individuals who come to embrace violent extremism.

Also since September 11, State and local law enforcement have received grant funding from the Federal Government to prepare and prevent terrorist activity. We saw the value of this grant funding after the bombing at last year's Boston Marathon as the police wore protective gear and stabilized the situation.

More recently, there was an example of what I believe to be an improper use of Federal equipment and resources in Ferguson, Missouri. Better oversight and tighter control of how Federal homeland security and law enforcement resources are used by State and local partners is one area that needs to be improved.

Another area that is a perennial challenge is information sharing with State and local law enforcement. Even with Fusion Centers and Joint Terrorist Task Forces, 13 years after September 11, we still hear that information sharing can be improved. Given threats from ISIL, al-Qaeda, lone-wolf actors and other terrorist organizations, is there a way to an optimal relationship between Federal, State, and local partners?

The 13 years since September 11 have shown us that we cannot have a myopic or narrow view of the terrorist threats we face. It is my hope that today we engage in a productive dialogue about the variety of threats to our Nation.

Thank you, and I yield back, Mr. Chairman.

[The statement of Ranking Member Thompson follows:]

STATEMENT OF RANKING MEMBER BENNIE G. THOMPSON

SEPTEMBER 17, 2014

We are fortunate to have an exceptionally accomplished and knowledgeable panel of witnesses to discuss the current threat picture. Secretary Johnson, welcome back. You have offered informative and useful testimony before, and I expect today to be no different. Director Comey, it is great to have the Bureau participate in today's discussion. I believe this is the first time we had an FBI director before the committee to testify. Hopefully, Mr. Chairman, we will have other opportunities to invite him back. Director Olsen, I join the Chairman in commending you for 24 years of Federal service and, in particular, your contributions as the director of the National Counterterrorism Center. I wish you the best during your transition.

Thirteen years ago this week, just days after the horrific September 11 terrorist attacks, then-President George W. Bush addressed Congress and the Nation. In his address, President Bush stated, "our war on terror begins with al-Qaeda and it will not end until every terrorist group of global reach has been found, stopped, and defeated". Thirteen years later, there have been some successes, particularly against core al-Qaeda, but as we know, not all terrorist groups have been "found, stopped, and defeated".

Those of us who were in the audience when President Bush delivered his address could not have predicted how the terrorist threat would evolve. At that time, Congress was completely focused on preventing another large-scale attack on U.S. soil. In 2001, we understood al-Qaeda to be a centralized organization. Little thought was given to the prospects that al-Qaeda would franchise terrorism and inspire satellite groups in the Arabian Peninsula and Africa.

The prospect that an attack would be carried out by a "lone-wolf actor" with no direct training or support from al-Qaeda barely entered the discussion. We were thinking that terrorist groups were focused on taking human lives; we did not predict that in the decade after September 11 state actors or terrorist groups would try to devastate our economy and steal valuable intellectual property by targeting our cyber infrastructure.

Finally, we could not have imagined that on the eve of the 13th anniversary of 9/11, another American President would come before the American people to make the case for defeating and destroying a terrorist organization. Indeed, the threat from the Islamic State of Iraq and the Levant (ISIL) is legitimate and warrants attention.

That said, the situation on the ground in Syria is fluid and complex; defeating and destroying ISIL in this context is no easy task. I cannot stress enough the need for vigilance and care, particularly should we decide to partner with individuals on the Syria to try and defeat ISIL. In addition to our efforts abroad, we need to remain vigilant and improve preparedness and resilience at home.

Last month's arrest of Don Morgan illustrates my long-standing view that we must reject specific ethnic or religious profiles of a "would-be terrorist". Violent extremism has no race, ethnicity, religion, or culture and there is no single profile or pathway for individuals who come to embrace violent extremism.

Also, since September 11, State and local law enforcement have received grant funding from the Federal Government to prepare for and prevent terrorist activity. We saw the value of this grant funding after the bombings at last year's Boston Marathon, as the police wore protective gear and stabilized the situation. More recently, there was an example of what I believe to be an improper use of Federal equipment and resources—in Ferguson, Missouri.

Better oversight and tighter control of how Federal homeland security and law enforcement resources are used by State and local partners is one area that needs to be improved. Another area that is a perennial challenge is information sharing with State and local law enforcement.

Even with fusion centers and joint terrorist task forces, 13 years after September 11, we still hear that information sharing can be improved. Given threats from ISIL, al-Qaeda, lone-wolf actors, and other terrorist organizations, is there a way to an optimal relationship between Federal, State, and local partners? The 13 years since September 11 have shown us that we cannot have a myopic or narrow view of the terrorist threats we face. It is my hope that today we engage in a productive dialogue about the variety of threats to our Nation.

Chairman MCCAUL. I thank the Ranking Member.

Other Members are reminded that opening statements may be submitted for the record.

We are pleased to have here today a distinguished panel of witnesses before us. First, Secretary Jeh Johnson, sworn in December 23, 2013 as the fourth Secretary of the Department of Homeland Security. Prior to joining DHS, Secretary Johnson served as general counsel for the Department of Defense where he was part of the senior management team and led more than 10,000 military and civilian lawyers across the Department.

He also oversaw the development of the legal aspects of many of our Nation's counterterrorism policies and spearheaded reforms to military commissions system at Guantanamo Bay in 2009.

Next, we are very pleased and honored to have to this committee for the first time Director James Comey. He became the seventh director of the Federal Bureau of Investigation in September 2013. Director Comey has a long history of service to the Department of Justice, including holding positions as both assistant U.S. attorney and U.S. attorney to the Southern District of New York, and assistant U.S. attorney for the Eastern District of Virginia, where I first met him when he was conducting Project Exile, a gun violence reduction initiative. I want to thank you for your efforts on that. He also served as deputy attorney general at the Justice Department.

Prior to his appointment, he held senior positions at Lockheed Martin and Bridgewater Associates.

Again, thank you so much for being here today.

Then, and last but not least, but it is his last appearance before this committee, but I am sure we will hear from him more times after this. But Director Matthew Olsen has served as director of the National Counterterrorism Center since August 2011. Prior to joining NCTC, Mr. Olsen served as the general counsel for the National Security Agency, where he was the chief legal officer for NSA and the principal legal adviser to the NSA director.

Director Olsen has a long record of service that includes time spent at the FBI, the Department of Justice, and the Guantanamo Review Task Force.

Again, we thank you for your service, sir.

The full written statements of each of the witnesses will appear in the record.

The Chairman now recognizes the Secretary of Homeland Security for his opening statement.

STATEMENT OF HON. JEH C. JOHNSON, SECRETARY, U.S. DEPARTMENT OF HOMELAND SECURITY

Secretary JOHNSON. Thank you, Chairman, Ranking Member Thompson. The committee has my prepared opening statement. I will not read it. I will just in a few moments here mention a couple of things.

One, thank you for holding this hearing. This is a very important hearing on a very important topic. This is just the type of public opportunity for Congressional oversight of our counterterrorism efforts that I welcome. This will not be my last appearance here, I am sure, and it is certainly not my first.

I want to say thank you to my friends and colleagues to my left and right for joining me. Director Comey and I have known each other for 25 years, when we were assistant U.S. attorneys together beginning in 1988, 1989. So I have known Jim for a very long time.

Matt Olsen I have known for 6 years now, going back to late 2008, early 2009. I hired Matt to be general counsel of NSA, along with General Alexander. He and I hired Matt to be general counsel of NSA. He did a terrific job there for a year, and he has been a terrific colleague in the National security-counterterrorism world. I and others will miss him very much for his clarity of delivery in terms of his intelligence assessments.

I mention my personal relationship with these two gentlemen to highlight the fact that homeland security, law enforcement, and the intelligence community have in my judgment a very, very good working relationship in dealing with counterterrorism matters. We are committed to working together on these issues. We are committed to information sharing. We are committed to collegiality. We are encouraging that among our staffs.

Just yesterday, Director Comey and I met with other members of the National security team in a periodic meeting to discuss National security topics. We do this often.

The other point I would like to make, Chairman, is ISIL is obviously the most prominent terrorist organization on the world stage right now. It is our focus. But from my homeland security perspective, and I am sure my colleagues share this, we have to stay focused on a range of terrorist threats. Al-Qaeda in the Arabian Peninsula, for example, is still active.

There are other threats emanating from that region, emanating from other parts of the world that we in homeland security-National security have to remain focused on. We have taken a number of steps in recent months to address aviation security, for example. You are aware of the enhancements that I directed in July and in August. We are addressing the issue of foreign fighters in and out of Syria, which I am sure we will discuss this morning, as well as, for example, enhanced countering violent extremism efforts here at home through various outreach programs that we have, including the pilot program the attorney general announced earlier this week.

So we are doing a number of things that we will be pleased to discuss with you at this morning's hearing. I look forward to your questions. Thank you again for holding this hearing.

[The prepared statement of Secretary Johnson follows:]

PREPARED STATEMENT OF JEH C. JOHNSON

SEPTEMBER 17, 2014

Chairman McCaul, Ranking Member Thompson, and Members of the committee: Thank you for the opportunity to appear today to discuss the Department of Homeland Security's (DHS) efforts to address world-wide threats to our homeland.

Before I begin, I would like to recognize my colleagues at the table: Federal Bureau of Investigation (FBI) Director Jim Comey and National Counterterrorism Center (NCTC) Director Matt Olsen. I have known both of these dedicated public servants for years. Twenty-five years ago Director Comey and I were assistant U.S. attorneys together in the Southern District of New York, and Matt Olsen was the general counsel of the NSA while I was the general counsel of the Defense Department. These two public servants are steadfast partners to DHS and to me, and I consider it a privilege to work alongside them as we meet our shared mission of keeping our Nation and the American people safe. As Matt prepares to leave his post at NCTC, I want to congratulate him on his 24 years of distinguished service to this country. As President Obama has said, every American is safer because of his service.

As this committee knows, the United States faces a constantly evolving threat environment. Thirteen years after the 9/11 attacks, threats to our Nation have not subsided.

The job of DHS and its more than 240,000 men and women is to remain vigilant against these threats, regardless of where they originate or what form they take. First and foremost, that means detecting and preventing terrorist threats that may seek to penetrate the homeland from land, sea, or air. As I have noted before, DHS must always be agile and vigilant in continually adapting to evolving threats, be it a foreign fighter or a "lone-wolf" terrorist living within our midst.

Counterterrorism is the cornerstone of the DHS mission. And 13 years after 9/11, it's still a dangerous world. There's still a terrorist threat to our homeland.

Today the terrorist threat is different from what it was in 2001. It is more decentralized and more complex. Not only is there core al-Qaeda in Afghanistan and Pakistan, there is al-Qaeda in the Arabian Peninsula—which is still active in its efforts to attack the homeland—al-Qaeda in the Islamic Maghreb, al-Shabaab in Somalia, the al-Nusrah Front in Syria, and the newest affiliate, al-Qaeda in the Indian subcontinent. There are groups like Boko Haram in Nigeria, which are not official affiliates of al-Qaeda, but share its extremist ideology.

The Islamic State of Iraq and the Levant, or ISIL, previously known as al-Qaeda in Iraq, is now vying to be the pre-eminent terrorist organization on the world's stage. At present, we have no credible information that ISIL is planning to attack the homeland of the United States.

But that is not, by any means, the end of the story.

ISIL is an extremely dangerous organization. It has the elements of both a terrorist organization and an insurgent army. It kills innocent civilians, and has seized large amounts of territory in Iraq and Syria, which it can utilize for safe haven, training, command and control, and from which it can launch attacks. It engages in 30–40 attacks per month, has more than 20,000 fighters, and takes in as much as a million dollars a day from illicit oil sales, ransom payments, and other illicit activities. Its public messaging and social media are as slick and as effective as any I've ever seen from a terrorist organization.

Though we know of no credible information that ISIL is planning to attack the homeland at present, we know that ISIL is prepared to kill innocent Americans they encounter because they are Americans—in a public and depraved manner. We know ISIL views the United States as an enemy, and we know that ISIL's leaders have themselves said they will soon be in "direct confrontation" with the United States.

On September 10, President Obama delivered a speech to the Nation in which he outlined this Government's response to ISIL.

The President has already begun a military campaign to take the fight to ISIL. To date, our military has launched well over 100 air strikes against ISIL in Iraq, to protect our personnel, critical infrastructure, and to support humanitarian activities there.

The United States will expand our efforts against ISIL, as part of a broad coalition of NATO allies and other allies in the region, reflecting the international community's condemnation of ISIL and its tactics. As part of this, we are pleased to see the formation of the new inclusive government in Iraq, with whom we intend to work closely. We look forward to this new government's addressing the rights and concerns of all of Iraq's diverse communities, and its leaders from across the political spectrum coming together to take a united stand against ISIL.

From the homeland security perspective, here is what we are doing:

First, to address the threats generally emanating from terrorist groups overseas, we have in recent weeks enhanced aviation security. Much of the terrorist threat continues to center around aviation security. In early July, I directed enhanced screening at 18 overseas airports with direct flights to the United States. Several weeks later, we added six more airports to the list. Three weeks ago we added another airport, and additional screening of carry-on luggage. The United Kingdom and other countries have followed with similar enhancements to their aviation security. We continually evaluate whether more is necessary, without unnecessarily burdening the traveling public.

Longer-term, as this committee has heard me say before, we are pursuing "pre-clearance" at overseas airports with flights to the United States. This means inspection by a U.S. Customs and Border Protection officer and enhanced aviation security before a passenger gets on the plane to the United States. We now have pre-clearance at airports in Ireland, the UAE, Canada, and the Caribbean. I regard it as a homeland security imperative to build more. To use a football metaphor, I'd much rather defend our end-zone from the 50-yard line than our 1-yard line. I want to take every opportunity we have to expand homeland security beyond our borders.

Second, the Department of Homeland Security, the FBI, NCTC, and other intelligence agencies are making enhanced and concerted efforts to track Syrian foreign fighters who come from or seek to enter this country. The reality is that more than 15,000 foreign fighters have traveled to Syria over the last 3 years, including approximately 2,000 Westerners. We estimate that more than 100 Americans have traveled or attempted to travel to Syria to join the fight there one way or another. We are concerned that not only may these foreign fighters join ISIL or other violent extremist groups in Syria, they may also be recruited by these violent extremist groups to leave Syria and conduct external attacks. The FBI has arrested a number of individuals who have tried to travel from the United States to Syria to support terrorist activities there.

Third, we are working with European and other governments to build better information sharing to track Syrian foreign fighters. Whenever I get together with my European counterparts, this topic is almost always item No. 1 on the agenda. The importance of this issue is also reflected by the fact it will be a singular topic of discussion at a U.N. Security Council summit that the President will chair in two weeks. In the history of the United Nations, this is only the second time a U.S. President has personally chaired a Security Council summit.

We are increasing efforts to track those who enter and leave Syria, and may later seek to travel to the United States from a country for which the United States does not require a visa from its citizens. There are in fact a number of Visa Waiver Program countries that also have large numbers of citizens who are Syrian foreign fighters. Generally, we have strong information-sharing relationships with these countries. But, with their help, we will enhance this capability. We need to ensure that we are doing all we can to identify those who, by their travel patterns, attempt to hide their association with terrorist groups.

We are encouraging more countries to join the United States in using tools like Advance Passenger Information and Passenger Name Record collection, which will help to identify terrorist travel patterns.

Fourth, within the U.S. Government, DHS and our interagency partners in law enforcement and the intelligence community, are enhancing our ability to share information with each other about suspicious individuals.

Fifth, we are continually on guard against the potential domestic-based, home-grown terrorist who may be lurking in our own society: The independent actor or "lone wolf" who did not train at a terrorist camp or join the ranks of a terrorist organization overseas, but who is inspired here at home by a group's social media, literature, or violent extremist ideology. In many respects, this is the hardest terrorist threat to detect, and the one I worry most about.

To address the domestic "lone-wolf" threat, I have directed that DHS build on our partnerships with State and local law enforcement in a way that enhances community relationships. The local police and fire departments are the first responders to any crisis in our homeland. The local police, more than the Federal Government, have their finger on the pulse of the local community from which a domestic terrorist may come.

To address the home-grown terrorist who may be lurking in our midst, we must also emphasize the need for help from the public. "If You See Something, Say Something" is more than a slogan. For example, last week we sent a private-sector advisory identifying for retail businesses a long list of materials that could be used as explosive precursors, and the types of suspicious behavior that a retailer should look for from someone who buys a lot of these materials.

Within DHS, we have outreach programs with communities who themselves are engaging youth in violence prevention. I have directed that we step up these programs and I personally participate in them. In June I met with a Syrian-American community group in a Chicago suburb. Next week I will meet with a Somali community in Columbus, Ohio. In October, the White House will host a summit on domestic efforts to prevent violent extremism, and address the full life cycle of radicalization to violence posed by foreign fighter threats. The efforts highlighted at this summit are meant to increase the participation of faith-based organizations, mental health providers, social service providers, and youth-affiliated groups in local efforts to counter violent extremism.

Over the last 13 years, we have vastly improved this Nation's ability to detect and disrupt terrorist plots overseas before they reach the homeland. Here at home, Federal law enforcement does an excellent job, time and again, of identifying, investigating, arresting, and prosecuting scores of individuals before they commit terrorist acts. But we continue to face real terrorist enemies and real terrorist threats and we must all remain vigilant.

As Secretary of Homeland Security, I see the full array of threats to our homeland every day, from the "lone wolf" to al-Qaeda affiliates like al-Qaeda in the Arabian Peninsula (which has made repeated efforts to export terrorism to our homeland) to ISIL and its ranks of foreign fighters.

As long as the world remains a dangerous place, as long as there are threats to the homeland in any form from any individual or group, the dedicated men and women of DHS will remain vigilant. We will take all the appropriate steps to continue to protect the homeland, in accordance with our fundamental rights and liberties, and in close partnership with our Federal, State, and local partners, the Congress, and the American people. Thank you.

Chairman MCCAUL. I thank the Secretary.

The Chairman now recognizes Director Comey for his testimony.

STATEMENT OF JAMES B. COMEY, DIRECTOR, FEDERAL BUREAU OF INVESTIGATION, U.S. DEPARTMENT OF JUSTICE

Mr. COMEY. Thank you, Mr. Chairman, Mr. Thompson. It is a pleasure to be before you for the first time and to be joined by my friends Jeh and Matt here at the table.

To Matt Olsen, the American people will never fully know how much he has done to keep them safe, but a lot of people in this room know and will be forever grateful.

Mr. Chairman, as you know, I was gone from Government for almost a decade, and so I have a perspective that may be different on the terrorist threat. When I came back to Government a year ago, I discovered the threat had changed in two ways that struck me. First, thanks largely to our men and women in uniform, we had taken the fight to the core al-Qaeda tumor in the Afghanistan-Pakistan region and shrunk that tumor in a significant way.

But at the same time, we had experienced a metastasis of that cancer, the progeny of al-Qaeda. This metastasis has sprung up in ungoverned or lightly-governed space in North Africa, the Gulf, the Mediterranean, in ways that are familiar to this committee.

The manifestation in Syria and Iraq is obviously a huge example of that metastasis. So that metastasis, coupled with the phenomenon of travelers seeking to go to those safe havens to get the experience of being a terrorist, to make those connections, is a way in which that change strikes me.

I am very concerned about the going. I am even more concerned about the coming. There will be a terrorist diaspora out of those areas, especially Syria, that we all wake up every day thinking and worrying about.

The second way in which the terrorism threat has changed has come with the way the internet has changed all of our lives. It is no longer necessary to actually meet somebody in al-Qaeda to get training and inspiration to conduct a terrorist attack here in the United States. Someone can do it in their pajamas in their basement.

These are the home-grown violent extremists that we worry about, who can get all the poison they need and the training they need to kill Americans, and in a way that is very hard for us to spot between the time they emerge from their basements and maybe kill innocent Americans. Those are the two ways in which I have seen the terrorism threat change significantly since I was last in Government.

Secretary Johnson mentioned cyber. All of us, as I have said, have connected our entire lives to the internet. It is where my children—I have five—it is where they play. It is where we bank. It is where my health care is. It is where critical infrastructure is. It is where my Nation's secrets are.

So that is where bad people come to do harm across those dimensions—people who want to hurt my kids, steal my identity, damage our infrastructure, steal our secrets, that is where they come. So to be effective, all of us need to be able to address those threats in cyber space. I think making sure the FBI is positioned, equipped, and trained to do that is going to dominate the 9 years I have left in my term.

It is an honor to be here to represent the people of the FBI. I believe I have the greatest job in the world, and it is a pleasure to be back in public service.

Thank you, sir.

[The prepared statement of Mr. Comey follows:]

PREPARED STATEMENT OF JAMES B. COMEY

SEPTEMBER 17, 2014

Good morning, Chairman McCaul, Ranking Member Thompson, and Members of the committee. Thank you for the opportunity to appear before you today to discuss the FBI's efforts to combat threats against the homeland.

Today's FBI is a threat-based, intelligence-driven organization. We live in a time of persistent terrorist and criminal threats to our National security, our economy, and to our communities. Just as our adversaries and threats continue to evolve, so, too, must the FBI. The key to this evolution lies with our greatest assets: Our people and our partnerships. Every FBI professional understands that thwarting the threats facing our Nation means constantly striving to be more effective and more efficient. The people of the FBI sacrifice much for their country, and I am proud to lead this organization of dedicated agents, analysts, and professional staff.

To accomplish its mission, the FBI relies heavily upon its law enforcement and intelligence partners around the Nation and around the globe.

By combining our resources and our collective expertise, we are able to investigate National security threats that cross both geographical and jurisdictional boundaries.

It is important to emphasize that the FBI carries out this broad mission with rigorous obedience to the rule of law and resolute respect for privacy, confidentiality, civil rights, and civil liberties of the citizens we serve.

COUNTERTERRORISM

Combating terrorism continues to be one of the top priorities for the FBI. As geopolitical conflict zones continue to emerge throughout many parts of the world, terrorist groups may use this instability to recruit and incite acts of violence.

While core al-Qaeda isn't the dominant force it once was, we have seen the growth of the al-Qaeda affiliates: al-Qaeda in the Islamic Maghreb, al-Qaeda in the Arabian Peninsula, al-Nusra Front in Syria, and now ISIL in Iraq and Syria.

Syria remains at the forefront of our minds as the on-going conflict shows no signs of subsiding. The continuing violence in both Syria and Iraq and the influx of foreign fighters threatens to further destabilize an already volatile region while also heightening the threat to the West. Due to the prolonged nature and the high visibility of the Syrian conflict, we are concerned that U.S. persons with an interest in committing violent extremist acts will continue to be drawn to the region. Foreign fighters traveling to Syria or Iraq could, for example, gain battlefield experience and increased exposure to violent extremist elements that may lead to further radicalization to violence; they may use these skills and exposure to radical ideology to return to their countries of origin, including the United States, to conduct attacks on the homeland. The FBI is working closely with our domestic and international partners to track foreign fighters traveling to the Middle East and to disrupt them before they act.

The Islamic State of Iraq and the Levant (ISIL) remains committed to instilling fear and attracting recruits. ISIL has issued public statements confirming the terrorist organization's determination and dedication to global terrorism. ISIL's widespread use of social media and growing on-line support intensified following the commencement of U.S. airstrikes in Iraq. ISIL has also shown the lengths to which it is willing to go to attract public attention. This was evident in the videos ISIL released depicting the beheadings of ISIL-held American hostages James Foley and Steven Sotloff. We are deeply concerned about the safety and security of American citizens world-wide, and ISIL and other foreign terrorist organizations may continue to try to capture American hostages in an attempt to force the U.S. Government and people into making concessions that would only strengthen ISIL and further its terrorist operations.

Al-Qaeda in the Arabian Peninsula (AQAP) remains one of the greatest threats to the United States. AQAP's intent on carrying out violent acts against the West is still strong. Through AQAP's on-line English magazine *Inspire,* the group advocates simple and inexpensive lone-wolf attacks against the homeland and other Western targets. The first edition of *Inspire,* released in the summer of 2010, provided specific instructions on how to build a pipe bomb. Last month, AQAP released a new publication that further expanded upon these instructions to include building a pressure cooker bomb similar to the one used in the Boston Marathon bombing.

Here at home, we face a continued threat from home-grown violent extremists (HVEs). HVEs are individuals located in the United States who are inspired by terrorist ideology. These individuals present unique challenges because they do not share the profile of an identifiable group. Their experience and motives are often distinct, but they are increasingly savvy and willing to act alone. They may gain inspiration from terrorist narratives, including material in English; events in the United States or abroad perceived as threatening to Muslims; the perceived success of other HVE plots, such as the November 2009 attack at Fort Hood; or their own grievances.

As you know, the FBI also relies heavily upon its 103 Joint Terrorism Task Forces (JTTFs) across the Nation. The FBI has added approximately 70 JTTFs since 9/11. Investigators, analysts, linguists, and experts from dozens of U.S. law enforcement and intelligence agencies comprise the JTTFs. The JTTFs serve as critical force multipliers that follow up on all terrorism leads, develop and investigate cases, and proactively identify threats and trends that may impact the region, the Nation, and the world.

Finally, in an effort to better address the evolving threat, the Countering Violent Extremism (CVE) Office uses FBI resources and works with Federal counterparts to empower our local partners to prevent violent extremists and their supporters from inspiring, radicalizing, financing, or recruiting individuals or groups in the United States to commit acts of violence.

Today's FBI remains agile in its efforts to combat National security threats both here and abroad. We are committed to utilizing all of our resources to protect the citizens of this country, and we will continue to further our integration of operations and intelligence to prevent acts of terrorism.

INTELLIGENCE

The FBI is a National security and law enforcement organization that uses, collects, and shares intelligence in everything we do.

There was a time when the FBI was criticized for "working the in-box." Our work was driven by sources and the complaints that came to our door. We too often worked what was directly in front of us, which didn't always align with our biggest threats or allow us to look beyond the horizon.

Today we are constantly involved in a process of trying to understand the threats we face in each of our offices here and abroad—what's out there, what we see, what we might be missing. We gather intelligence, consistent with our authorities, to help us understand and rank those threats and to identify the intelligence gaps we face. We then try to fill those gaps and continue to learn as much as we can about the threats we are addressing and those we may need to address. We do this for National security and criminal threats, Nationally and within each field office. We then compare the National and local perspectives to develop a threat prioritization ranking for each of the FBI's 56 field offices. By creating this ranking, we strive to actively pursue our highest threats. This gives us a better assessment of what the dangers are, what's being done about them, and what we should spend time on.

The FBI has come a long way in its intelligence transformation over the years, but there is always room to improve and grow. We have reinstituted the FBI's Intelligence Branch to elevate and expand the intelligence program. I am confident that this will result in a more robust FBI with continued integration of intelligence and operations. I also anticipate the expansion will facilitate a smoother, more efficient exchange of intelligence with the intelligence community and international partners.

CYBER

We face cyber threats from state-sponsored hackers, hackers for hire, global cyber syndicates, and terrorists. They seek our state secrets, our trade secrets, our technology, and our ideas—things of incredible value to all of us. They seek to strike our critical infrastructure and to harm our economy.

Given the scope of the cyber threat, agencies across the Federal Government are making cybersecurity a top priority. The Department of Justice, including the FBI; the Department of Homeland Security; the National Security Agency and other U.S. intelligence community and law enforcement agencies have truly undertaken a whole-of-Government effort to combat the cyber threat. Within the FBI, we are prioritizing the investigation and prevention of high-level intrusions against the United States, including the biggest and most dangerous botnets, state-sponsored hackers, and global cyber syndicates. We are working with our counterparts to predict and prevent attacks, rather than simply react after the fact.

FBI agents, analysts, and computer scientists use technical capabilities and traditional investigative techniques—such as sources and wiretaps, surveillance, and forensics—to fight cyber crime. We work side-by-side with our Federal, State, and local partners on Cyber Task Forces in each of our 56 field offices and at the National Cyber Investigative Joint Task Force (NCIJTF). Through our 24-hour cyber command center, CyWatch, we combine the resources of the FBI and NCIJTF, allowing us to provide connectivity to Federal cyber centers, Government agencies, FBI field offices and legal attachés, and the private sector in the event of a cyber intrusion.

We also exchange information about cyber threats with the private sector through partnerships such as the Domestic Security Alliance Council, InfraGard, and the National Cyber Forensics and Training Alliance (NCFTA).

We developed and recently deployed a malware repository and analysis system called Malware Investigator (MI) for intelligence and law enforcement partners. MI provides the FBI's domestic and foreign law enforcement partners as well as members of the intelligence community a way to submit malware directly to the FBI. This approach will enable the FBI to obtain a global view of the malware threat, while also providing the submitter technical information about the malware's functionality. Beyond technical reporting, MI identifies correlations that will allow users to "connect the dots" by highlighting instances in which malware was deployed in seemingly unrelated incidents. MI will be provided to FBI corporate and academic partners later this year, providing them a trusted venue in which to investigate, analyze, study, and collaborate about malware threats.

In addition, our legal attaché offices overseas work to coordinate cyber investigations and address jurisdictional hurdles and differences in the law from country to country. We are supporting and collaborating with newly-established cyber crime centers at Interpol and Europol. We continue to assess other locations to ensure that our cyber personnel are in the most appropriate locations across the globe.

Over the past several months, the Justice Department has announced a series of separate indictments of overseas cyber criminals. In an unprecedented indictment in May, we charged five Chinese hackers with illegally penetrating the networks of six U.S. companies. The five members of China's People's Liberation Army allegedly used their illegal access to exfiltrate proprietary information, including trade secrets. Moreover, in June, charges were filed against Su Bin, a Chinese national, stemming from a computer hacking scheme that involved the theft of trade secrets from American defense contractors, including The Boeing Company, which manufactures the C–17 military transport aircraft.

Through the NCIJTF and in alliance with its U.S. Government partners, international partners, and private-sector stakeholders, the FBI has worked collaboratively in developing a multi-pronged effort aimed at defeating the world's most dangerous botnets. Over the past several years, the FBI's efforts to combat these significant cyber threats have caused the disruption and dismantlement of numerous botnets, including Butterfly Bot, Rove Digital, Coreflood, ZeroAccess, and GameOver Zeus, resulting in numerous arrests, extraditions, and convictions.

In addition to these recent investigative successes against the threat, we are continuing to work with our partners to prevent attacks before they occur. One area in which we have had great success with our overseas partners is in targeting infrastructure we believe has been used in distributed denial of service (DDoS) attacks, and preventing that infrastructure from being used for future attacks.

Since October 2012, the FBI and the Department of Homeland Security (DHS) have released more than 170,000 Internet Protocol addresses of computers that were believed to be infected with DDoS malware. We have released this information through Joint Indicator Bulletins (JIBs) to more than 130 countries via DHS's National Cybersecurity and Communications Integration Center (NCCIC), where our liaisons provide expert and technical advice for increased coordination and collaboration, as well as to our legal attachés overseas.

Chairman McCaul, Ranking Member Thompson, and the committee, I thank you for this opportunity to testify concerning the diverse threats facing the Nation and the FBI's on-going efforts to combat them. I am now happy to answer any questions you might have.

Chairman MCCAUL. Well, thank you. It is certainly a pleasure to have you here today as well. I forgot that we share the fact that we both have five children on social media, which can always be challenging at times.

With that, the Chairman now recognizes Director Olsen.

STATEMENT OF MATTHEW G. OLSEN, DIRECTOR, NATIONAL COUNTERTERRORISM CENTER

Mr. OLSEN. Thank you very much. Good morning, Chairman, Mr. Thompson, Members of the committee. Thank you for inviting me here this morning.

We often meet in closed Classified sessions, so this is a really important opportunity for us to speak to the committee in an open session and to the American people about the threats we face. I also want to say to you, Chairman, and to the rest of the committee, how much on behalf of the men and women of the National Counterterrorism Center we appreciate the committee's support in our efforts.

I will spend just a couple of minutes talking about the threat from Iraq and Syria and then take a moment to talk about how that threat fits into the broader terrorism landscape that we see.

First, by every measure, ISIL has emerged as an extremely dangerous organization in a very chaotic part of the world. The group has exploited the civil war in Syria, it has taken advantage of sectarian tensions in Iraq to entrench itself in both countries.

It has established sanctuaries in Iraq and in Syria. From where the group has the ability to plan and to train and also to amass both fighters and weapons with really little interference.

The group has proven to be an effective fighting force. It's battlefield strategy is complex and it is adaptive. It uses a mix of techniques from terrorist operations to hit-and-run tactics, to paramilitary assaults to enable their recent gains. Then importantly, the group also views itself as the now leader of a global jihadist movement. It operates the most sophisticated propaganda machine of any terrorist organization. It turns out timely, high-quality media, and it uses social media to secure a wide-spread following.

Today, we believe that ISIL has as many as 30,000-plus fighters and controls much of the Tigris-Euphrates basin, which is a crossroads of the Middle East. From this position, ISIL poses a multifaceted threat to the United States.

This past January, the leader of ISIL warned that U.S.—the United States will soon be in direct conflict with the group. There is little doubt that ISIL views us—views the United States as a strategic enemy.

This threat to us is most acute in Iraq. The group's safe haven and resources in Iraq pose an immediate and direct threat to our presence there, particularly our embassy in Baghdad and, of course, that threat includes the threat to Americans held hostage by ISIL.

The death threat extends outside of Iraq to the West. ISIL has the potential to use its safe haven and to plan, in coordinated attacks, both in Europe and potentially in the United States. This threat became real earlier this year, with the shooting in a Brussels museum that killed four people by an ISIL fighter. Then with the arrest we saw in France of an ISIL operative who had access to several explosive devices.

At this point, we have no information that ISIL is plotting an attack inside the United States. But we do know, as my colleague said, Director Comey and Secretary Johnson have referred to, that thousands of foreign fighters have flocked to Syria over the past 3 years. This includes more than 2,000 Europeans and more than a hundred Americans.

Many of these fighters that have flocked to Syria have joined ISIL's ranks. We are concerned, of course, that these fighters will gain experience, training, and eventually return to their home countries, battle-hardened and radicalized, some possessing Western passports and travel documents.

We are also concerned about the possibility of a home-grown extremist becoming radicalized by the information that is on the internet and carrying out a limited self-directed attack here at home for which we would have—we would face potentially little or no warning.

So second, this phenomenon, the rise of ISIL, exemplifies the threat and the transformation of the terrorism threat that we have seen over the past several years. We have seen this movement diversify and expand in the aftermath of the upheaval and chaos in the Arab world since 2010. So as my colleagues have mentioned,

ISIL is just one of the groups that we are concerned about. Al-Qaeda core continues to support attacking the West and, for now, remains the recognized leader of a global jihadist movement.

In Syria, we have seen veteran al-Qaeda fighters travel from Pakistan to take advantage of the permissive environment there. Al-Qaeda's official branches in Yemen and Somalia continue to remain extremely active. Of course, over the past 5 years, al-Qaeda in the Arabian Peninsula sought on three times to take down an airplane bound for the United States. Then here in the United States, last year's bombing of the Boston Marathon is a reminder, a sober reminder of the threat we face from self-directed violent extremists.

So terrorist networks have exploited the lack of governance and the lax security in parts of the Middle East and North Africa. Terrorist groups are now active in at least 11 insurgencies in the Islamic world.

The final point I will make on this is that identifying and disrupting these threats is increasingly challenging. The groups are adapting their tactics to overcome our defenses, to avoid our intelligence collection. They are looking for simpler, less sophisticated attacks that are on a smaller scale and that are easier to pull off, such as the al-Shabaab attack at the Westgate Mall last year in Nairobi.

Then finally, following the disclosure of the stolen NSA documents, terrorists are changing how they communicate. They are moving to more secure communication platforms. They are adopting encryption and they are avoiding electronic communications altogether. We see this in our reporting. This is a problem for us in many areas where we have limited human collection and depend on intercepting communications to identify terrorists and disrupt plots.

Members of the committee, to counter this threat, the men and women at NCTC remain vigilant around the clock. We are dedicated to working with our counterterrorism partners, particularly the FBI and DHS, to identify these threats, degrade networks and disrupt plots, both at home and abroad. We appreciate the committee's continued support. Thank you again for this opportunity. I look forward to your questions.

[The prepared statement of Mr. Olsen follows:]

PREPARED STATEMENT OF MATTHEW G. OLSEN

SEPTEMBER 17, 2014

Thank you Chairman McCaul, Ranking Member Thompson, and Members of the committee. I appreciate this opportunity to be here today to discuss the terrorist threat against the United States and our efforts to counter it.

As I conclude 3 years as director of the National Counterterrorism Center, I also want to express my deep appreciation to the committee for its unflagging support of the men and women at the National Counterterrorism Center and our counterterrorism community, as a whole. I am also particularly pleased to be here today with Secretary of Homeland Security Jeh Johnson and FBI Director James Comey. DHS and the FBI are two of our closest partner agencies. Together we are a part of the broader counterterrorism effort that is more integrated and more collaborative than ever.

Earlier this summer the 9/11 Commissioners released their most recent report, and asked National security leaders to "communicate to the public—in specific terms—what the threat is, and how it is evolving." Hearings like this provide an opportunity to continue this dialogue with the public and their elected representatives.

In May, the President told the graduating class of West Point cadets, "For the foreseeable future, the most direct threat to America at home and abroad remains terrorism." The 9/11 Commissioners agreed, noting in their July report, "the terrorist threat is evolving, not defeated." From my vantage point at the National Counterterrorism Center, I would agree. Since we testified before this committee last year, the terrorist threat has continued to evolve, becoming more geographically diffuse and involving a greater diversity of actors.

Overseas, the United States faces an enduring threat to our interests. We have adopted precautionary measures at some of our overseas installations. The threat emanates from a broad geographic area, spanning South Asia, across the Middle East, and much of North Africa, where terrorist networks have exploited a lack of governance and lax security.

Here in the United States, last year's attack against the Boston Marathon highlighted the danger posed by lone actors and insular groups not directly tied to terrorist organizations, as well as the difficulty of identifying these types of plots before they take place. The flow of more than 15,000 foreign fighters to Syria with varying degrees of access to Europe and the United States heightens our concern, as these individuals may eventually return to their home countries battle-hardened, radicalized, and determined to attack us.

In the face of sustained counterterrorism pressure, core al-Qaeda has adapted by becoming more decentralized and is shifting away from large-scale, mass casualty plots like the attacks of September 11, 2001. Al-Qaeda has modified its tactics, encouraging its adherents to adopt simpler attacks that do not require the same degree of resources, training, and planning.

Instability in the Levant, Middle East, and across North Africa has accelerated this decentralization of the al-Qaeda movement, which is increasingly influenced by local and regional factors and conditions. This diffusion has also led to the emergence of new power centers and an increase in threats by networks of like-minded violent extremists with allegiances to multiple groups. Ultimately, this less-centralized network poses a more diverse and geographically-dispersed threat and is likely to result in increased low-level attacks against U.S. and European interests overseas.

Today, I will begin by examining the terrorist threats to the homeland and then outline the threat to U.S. interests overseas, including from the Islamic State in Iraq and the Levant (ISIL). I will then focus the remainder of my remarks on some of NCTC's efforts to address this complicated threat picture.

Starting with the homeland, terrorist groups continue to target Western aviation. In early July, the United States and United Kingdom implemented enhanced security measures at airports with direct flights to the United States, which included new rules aimed at screening personal electronic devices. This past winter, we implemented additional security measures for commercial aviation to address threats to the Sochi Olympics. Although unrelated, taken together these two instances reflect the fact that terrorist groups continue to see commercial aviation as a desirable symbolic target,

Al-Qaeda in the Arabian Peninsula (AQAP) remains the al-Qaeda affiliate most likely to attempt transnational attacks against the United States. The group's repeated efforts to conceal explosive devices to destroy aircraft demonstrate its long-standing interest in targeting Western aviation. Its three attempted attacks demonstrate the group's continued pursuit of high-profile attacks against the West, its awareness of security procedures, and its efforts to adapt.

Despite AQAP's ambitions, home-grown violent extremists (HVEs) remain the most likely immediate threat to the homeland. The overall level of HVE activity has been consistent over the past several years: A handful of uncoordinated and unsophisticated plots emanating from a pool of up to a few hundred individuals. Lone actors or insular groups who act autonomously pose the most serious HVE threat, and we assess HVEs will likely continue gravitating to simpler plots that do not require advanced skills, outside training, or communications with others.

The Boston Marathon bombing underscores the threat from HVEs who are motivated to act violently by themselves or in small groups. In the months prior to the attack, the Boston Marathon bombers exhibited few behaviors that law enforcement and intelligence officers traditionally use to detect readiness to commit violence. The perceived success of previous lone offender attacks—combined with al-Qaeda's and AQAP's propaganda promoting individual acts of terrorism—is raising the profile of this tactic.

HVEs make use of an on-line environment that is dynamic, evolving, and self-sustaining. This on-line environment is likely to play a critical role in the foreseeable future in radicalizing and mobilizing HVEs towards violence. Despite the removal of important terrorist leaders during the last several years, the on-line outlets continue to reinforce a violent extremist identity, highlight grievances, and provide HVEs the means to connect with terrorist groups overseas.

This boundless virtual environment, combined with terrorists' increasingly sophisticated use of social media, makes it increasingly difficult to protect our youth from propaganda. ISIL's on-line media presence has become increasingly sophisticated, disseminating timely, high-quality media content across multiple platforms.

THE ISLAMIC STATE OF IRAQ AND THE LEVANT (ISIL)

ISIL is a terrorist organization that has exploited the conflict in Syria and sectarian tensions in Iraq to entrench itself in both countries. The group's strength, which we estimate may include more than 30,000 members—as well as its expansionary agenda—pose an increasing threat to our regional allies and to U.S. facilities and personnel in both the Middle East and the West.

ISIL's goal is to solidify and expand its control of territory and govern by implementing its violent interpretation of sharia law. The group aspires to overthrow governments in the region, govern all the territory that the early Muslim caliphs controlled, and expand. ISIL's claim to have re-established the caliphate reflects the group's desire to lead violent extremists around the world.

ISIL exploited the conflict and chaos in Syria to expand its operations across the border. The group, with al-Qaeda's approval, established the al-Nusrah Front in late 2011 as a cover for its Syria-based activities but in April 2013, unilaterally declared its presence in Syria under the ISIL name. ISIL accelerated its efforts to overthrow the Iraqi government, seizing control of Fallujah this past January. The group expanded from its safe haven in Syria and across the border into northern Iraq, killing thousands of Iraqi Muslims on its way to seizing Mosul this June.

Along the way, ISIL aggressively recruited new adherents. In Syria, some joined ISIL to escape Assad's brutal treatment and oppression of the Syrian people. Others in Iraq joined out of frustration, marginalized by their own government. But many joined out of intimidation and fear, forced to choose either obedience to ISIL or a violent death.

The withdrawal of Iraqi Security Forces during those initial military engagements has left ISIL with large swaths of ungoverned territory. The group has established sanctuaries in Syria and Iraq from where it plans, trains, and plots terrorist acts with little interference. We assess ISIL's strength has increased and reflects stronger recruitment this summer following battlefield successes, the declaration of a caliphate, and additional intelligence. ISIL's freedom of movement over the Iraq-Syria border enables the group to easily move members between Iraq and Syria, which can rapidly change the number of fighters in either country. ISIL is also drawing some recruits from the more than 15,000 foreign fighters who have traveled to Syria.

ISIL's recent victories have provided the group with a wide array of weapons, equipment, and other resources. Battlefield successes also have given ISIL an extensive war chest, which as of early this month probably includes around $1 million per day in revenues from black-market oil sales, smuggling, robberies, looting, extortion, and ransom payments for hostages. While ISIL receives some funding from outside donors, this pales in comparison to its self-funding through criminal and terrorist activities.

ISIL has sought to question the legitimacy of Ayman al-Zawahiri's succession of Usama bin Ladin. While al-Qaeda core remains the ideological leader of the global terrorist movement, its primacy is being challenged by the rise of ISIL whose territorial gains, increasing access to a large pool of foreign fighters, and brutal tactics are garnering significantly greater media attention. We continue to monitor signs of fracturing within al-Qaeda's recognized affiliates.

ISIL's safe haven in Syria and Iraq and the group's access to resources pose an immediate and direct threat to U.S. personnel and facilities in the region. This includes our embassy in Baghdad and our consulate in Erbil—and, of course, it includes the Americans held hostage by ISIL.

But ISIL's threat extends beyond the region, to the West. This January, ISIL's leader publicly threatened "direct confrontation" with the United States, and has repeatedly taunted Americans, most recently through the execution of two American journalists who were reporting on the plight of the Syrian people, and one British aid worker. In Europe, the May 2014 shooting in Brussels by an ISIL-trained French national and the separate, earlier arrest of an ISIL-connected individual in France who possessed several explosive are two examples that demonstrate this threat, and the overall threat posed by returning foreign fighters.

In the United States, the FBI has arrested more than half a dozen individuals seeking to travel from the United States to Syria to join the fighting there, possibly with ISIL. We remain mindful of the possibility that an ISIL-sympathizer could conduct a limited, self-directed attack here at home with no warning.

AL-QAEDA CORE AND AFGHANISTAN/PAKISTAN-BASED GROUPS

Turning to core al-Qaeda and Afghanistan/Pakistan-based groups, we anticipate that despite core al-Qaeda's diminished leadership cadre, remaining members will continue to pose a threat to Western interests in South Asia and would attempt to strike the homeland should an opportunity arise. Al-Qaeda leader Ayman al-Zawahiri's public efforts to promote individual acts of violence in the West have increased, as the Pakistan-based group's own capabilities have diminished.

Despite ISIL's challenge, Zawahiri remains the recognized leader of the global jihadist movement among al-Qaeda affiliates and allies, and the groups continue to defer to his guidance on critical issues. Since the start of the Arab unrest in North Africa and the Middle East, Zawahiri and other members of the group's leadership have directed their focus there, encouraging cadre and associates to support and take advantage of the unrest.

Al-Qaeda in the Indian Subcontinent.—This month, al-Qaeda announced the establishment of its newest affiliate, al-Qaeda in the Indian Subcontinent (AQIS). Al-Qaeda used social media and on-line web forums to make known the existence of AQIS, which al-Qaeda said it has worked for more than 2 years to create. We assess the creation of AQIS is not a reaction to al-Qaeda's split with ISIL, though the timing of the announcement may be used to bolster al-Qaeda's standing in the global jihad movement. AQIS, which is led by Sheikh Asim Umer, has stated objectives that include violence against the United States, establishing Islamic law in South Asia, ending occupation of Muslim lands, and defending Afghanistan under Mullah Omar's leadership. AQIS on 11 September publicly claimed responsibility for a thwarted September attack on a Pakistani Naval vessel at the Karachi Naval Dockyard. The group had planned to use the attack to target a U.S. Navy ship. AQIS also claimed responsibility for the killing of a senior Pakistani Inter-Services Intelligence officer earlier this month.

South Asia-Based Militants.—Pakistani and Afghan militant groups—including Tehrik-e Taliban Pakistan (TTP), the Haqqani Network, and Lashkar-e-Tayyiba (LT)—continue to pose a direct threat to U.S. interests and our allies in the region, where these groups probably will remain focused. We continue to watch for indicators that any of these groups, networks, or individuals are actively pursuing or have decided to incorporate operations outside of South Asia as a strategy to achieve their objectives.

TTP remains a significant threat in Pakistan despite the on-going Pakistan military operations in North Waziristan and leadership changes during the past year. Its claim of responsibility for the June attack on the Jinnah International Airport in Karachi that killed about 30 people underscores the threat the group poses inside the country.

The Haqqani network is one of the most capable and lethal terrorist groups in Afghanistan and poses a serious threat to the stability of the Afghan state as we approach 2014 and beyond. Last month, the Department of State listed four high-ranking Haqqani members—Aziz Haqqani, Khalil Haqqani, Yahya Haqqani, and Qari Abdul Rauf—on the "Rewards for Justice" most-wanted list for their involvement in terrorist attacks in Afghanistan and ties to al-Qaeda. The Haqqanis have conducted numerous high-profile attacks against United States, NATO, Afghan Government, and other allied nation targets. In October 2013, Afghan security forces intercepted a truck bomb deployed by the Haqqanis against Forward Operating Base Goode in the Paktiya Province. The device, which did not detonate, contained some 61,500 pounds of explosives and constitutes the largest truck bomb ever recovered in Afghanistan.

Lashkar-e-Tayyiba (LT) remains focused on its regional goals in South Asia. The group is against improving relations between India and Pakistan, and its leaders consistently speak out against India and the United States, accusing both countries of trying to destabilize Pakistan. LT has attacked Western interests in South Asia in pursuit of its regional objectives, as demonstrated by the targeting of hotels frequented by Westerners during the Mumbai attacks in 2008. LT leaders almost certainly recognize that an attack on the United States would result in intense international backlash against Pakistan and endanger the group's safe haven there. However, LT also provides training to Pakistani and Western militants, some of whom could plot terrorist attacks in the West without direction from LT leadership.

AL-QAEDA AFFILIATES

AQAP.—Al-Qaeda in the Arabian Peninsula (AQAP) remains the affiliate most likely to attempt transnational attacks against the United States. AQAP's three attempted attacks against the United States to date—the airliner plot of December 2009, an attempted attack against U.S.-bound cargo planes in October 2010, and an airliner plot in May 2012—demonstrate the group's continued pursuit of high-profile attacks against the United States. In a propaganda video released in March, the group's leader threatened the United States in a speech to recruits in Yemen, highlighting AQAP's persistent interest in targeting the United States.

AQAP also presents a high threat to U.S. personnel and facilities in Yemen and Saudi Arabia. In response to credible al-Qaeda threat reporting in August 2013, the State Department issued a global travel alert and closed U.S. embassies in the Middle East and North Africa as part of an effort to take precautionary steps against such threats. We assess that we at least temporarily delayed this particular plot, but we continue to track closely the status of AQAP plotting against our facilities and personnel in Yemen. AQAP continues to kidnap Westerners in Yemen and carry out numerous small-scale attacks and large-scale operations against Yemeni government targets, demonstrating the range of the group's capabilities. In addition, this past July AQAP launched its first successful attack in Saudi Arabia since 2009, underscoring the group's continued focus on operations in the Kingdom.

Finally, AQAP continues its efforts to radicalize and mobilize to violence individuals outside Yemen through the publication of its English-language magazine *Inspire.* Following the Boston Marathon bombings, AQAP released a special edition of the magazine claiming that accused bombers Tamarlan and Dzhokhar Tsarnaev were "inspired by *Inspire,*" highlighting the attack's simple, repeatable nature, and tying it to alleged U.S. oppression of Muslims world-wide. The most recent *Inspire* issue in March—AQAP's twelfth—continued to encourage "lone offender" attacks in the West, naming specific targets in the United States, United Kingdom, and France and providing instructions on how to construct a vehicle-borne improvised explosive device.

Al-Nusrah Front.—Al-Nusrah Front has mounted suicide, explosive, and firearms attacks against regime and security targets across the country; it has also sought to provide limited public services and governance to the local population in areas under its control. Several Westerners have joined al-Nusrah Front, including a few who have perished in suicide operations, raising concerns capable individuals with extremist contacts and battlefield experience could return to their home countries to commit violence. In April 2013, al-Nusrah Front's leader, Abu Muhammad al-Jawlani, pledged allegiance to al-Qaeda leader Ayman al-Zawahiri, publicly affirming the group's ties to core al-Qaeda. Al-Zawahiri named the group al-Qaeda's recognized affiliate in the region later last year, ordering ISIL to return to Iraq.

Al-Shabaab.—Al-Shabaab and its foreign fighter cadre are a potential threat to the U.S. homeland, as some al-Shabaab leaders have publicly called for transnational attacks and the group has attracted dozens of U.S. persons—mostly ethnic Somalis—who have traveled to Somalia since 2006. A recent U.S. military airstrike killed al-Shabaab's leader, Ahmed Abdi. This removes a capable leader of the group, but also raises the possibility of potential retaliatory attacks against our personnel and facilities in East Africa.

Al-Shabaab is mainly focused on undermining the Somali Federal Government and combating African Mission in Somalia (AMISOM) and regional military forces operating in Somalia. While al-Shabaab's mid-September 2013 attack on the Westgate mall in Kenya demonstrated that the group continues to plot against regional and Western targets across East Africa, as part of its campaign to remove foreign forces aiding the Somali Government.

AQIM and Regional Allies.—Al-Qaeda in the Lands of the Islamic Maghreb (AQIM) and its allies remain focused on local and regional attack plotting, including targeting Western interests. The groups have shown minimal interest in targeting the U.S. homeland.

In Mali, the French-led military intervention has pushed AQIM and its allies from the cities that they once controlled, but the groups maintain safe haven in the less-populated areas of northern Mali from which they are able to plan and launch attacks against French and allied forces in the region. Elsewhere, AQIM is taking advantage of permissive operating environments across much of North Africa to broaden its reach. We are concerned that AQIM may be collaborating with local violent extremists, including Ansar al-Sharia groups in Libya and Tunisia.

In August of last year, two highly-capable AQIM offshoots, Mokhtar Belmokhtar's al-Mulathamun battalion and Tawhid Wal Jihad in West Africa, merged to form the new violent extremist group-al-Murabitun—which will almost certainly seek to conduct additional high-profile attacks against Western interests across the region. Belmokhtar—the group's external operations commander——played a leading role in attacks against Western interests in Northwest Africa in 2013, with his January attack on an oil facility in In-Amenas, Algeria and double suicide bombings in Niger in May. Early this year, Belmokhtar relocated from Mali to Libya to escape counterterrorism pressure, and probably to collaborate with Ansar al-Sharia (AAS) and other violent extremist elements in the country to advance his operational goals.

Boko Haram.—While Boko Haram is not an official al-Qaeda affiliate, the group is waging unprecedented violence in northeast Nigeria this year and is expanding its reach into other parts of Nigeria and neighboring states to implement its harsh version of sharia law and suppress the Nigerian government and regional CT pressure. Since late 2012, Boko Haram and its splinter faction Ansaru have claimed responsibility for five kidnappings of Westerners, raising their international profile and highlighting the threat they pose to Western and regional interests, although Ansaru has not claimed an operation since Feburary 2013. Boko Haram has kidnapped scores of additional Nigerians in northeast Nigeria since the kidnapping of 276 school girls from Chibok, Nigeria in April 2014.

THREAT FROM SHIA GROUPS

Iran and Hizballah remain committed to defending the Assad regime, including sending billions of dollars in military and economic aid, training pro-regime and Shia militants, and deploying their own personnel into the country. Iran and Hizballah view the Assad regime as a key partner in an "axis of resistance" against Israel and the West and are prepared to take major risks to preserve the regime as well as their critical transshipment routes.

Lebanese Hizballah.—In May of last year, Hizballah publicly admitted that it is fighting for the Syrian regime and its chief, Hasan Nasrallah, framed the war as an act of self-defense against Western-backed Sunni violent extremists. Hizballah continues sending capable fighters for pro-regime operations and support for a pro-regime militia. Additionally, Iran and Hizballah are leveraging allied Iraqi Shi'a militant and terrorist groups to participate in counter-opposition operations. This active support to the Assad regime is driving increased Sunni violent extremist attacks and sectarian unrest in Lebanon.

Beyond its role in Syria, Lebanese Hizballah remains committed to conducting terrorist activities world-wide and we remain concerned the group's activities could either endanger or target U.S. and other Western interests. The group has engaged in an aggressive terrorist campaign in recent years and continues attack planning abroad. In April 2014, two Hizballah operatives were arrested in Thailand and one admitted that they were there to carry out a bomb attack against Israeli tourists, underscoring the threat to civilian centers.

Iranian Threat.—In addition to its role in Syria, Iran remains the foremost state sponsor of terrorism, and works through the Islamic Revolutionary Guard Corps-Quds Force and Ministry of Intelligence and Security to support groups that target U.S. and Israeli interests globally. In March, Israel interdicted a maritime vessel that departed Iran and was carrying munitions judged to be intended for Gaza-based Palestinian militants. Iran, largely through Quds Force Commander Soleimani, has also provided support to Shia militias and the Iraqi government to combat ISIL in Iraq.

Iran continues to be willing to conduct terrorist operations against its adversaries. This is demonstrated by Iran's links to terrorist operations in Azerbaijan, Georgia, India, and Thailand in 2012. Iran also continues to provide lethal aid and support the planning and execution of terrorist acts by other groups, in particular Lebanese Hizballah.

NCTC'S MISSIONS AND INITIATIVES

NCTC serves as the primary U.S. Government organization for analyzing and integrating all terrorism information. Now in our 10th year of service, we are guided by our mission statement: "Lead our Nation's effort to combat terrorism at home and abroad by analyzing the threat, sharing that information with our partners, and integrating all instruments of National power to ensure unity of effort."

Intelligence Integration and Analysis.—NCTC has a unique responsibility for the U.S. Government to examine all international terrorism issues, spanning geographic boundaries to identify and analyze threat information, regardless of whether it is collected inside or outside the United States.

Leading the Intelligence Community's Terrorism Warning Program.—NCTC chairs the Interagency Intelligence Committee on Terrorism (IICT), which is the IC's terrorism warning body. The IICT—which is comprised of the CIA, DHS, DIA, FBI, NCTC, NGA, NSA, and DOS—is responsible for the publication of products that warn of threats against U.S. personnel, facilities, or interests. The IICT serves several thousand customers, from senior policymakers, to deployed military forces and State and local law enforcement entities.

Watchlisting and TIDE.—As you know, this committee and the Congress charged NCTC with maintaining the U.S. Government's central and shared knowledge bank of known and suspected international terrorists (or KSTs), their contacts, and their support networks. To manage this workload, NCTC developed a database called TIDE—the Terrorist Identities Datamart Environment. Through TIDE, NCTC advances the most complete and accurate information picture to our partners in support of terrorism identities analysis, travel screening, and watchlisting activities.

The Kingfisher Expansion visa counterterrorism screening process for U.S. visa applicants successfully launched in June 2013 and provides a secure on-line vetting platform for FBI, DHS, and the Terrorism Screening Center to participate in the review of applicants. This process allows for a more comprehensive and coordinated response back to the State Department. To date, this program has conducted the review of more than 11 million visa applications.

In addition, in the last year, NCTC—in coordination with DHS—deployed the Kingfisher Expansion Electronic System for Travel Authorization (ESTA) program. NCTC has been providing screening support on ESTA applicants since 2010, however, the new interface provides NCTC analysts with a streamlined method of performing identity resolution on potential matches and provides a means for matches to be automatically populated into DHS' National Targeting Center-Passenger's ESTA Hotlist.

Situational Awareness and Support to Counterterrorism Partners.—NCTC—via the NCTC Operations Center and Joint Counterterrorism Assessment Team (JCAT)—is engaged 24/7/365 as the eyes and ears of the U.S. Government's global counterterrorism situational awareness effort. The Operations Center uses unique accesses and works with collocated assets, personnel, and resources from across the intelligence community to identify, track, and share key threat reporting streams and information with appropriate audiences in a timely fashion at a variety of classification levels.

JCAT complements the Operations Center's situational awareness efforts by building collaborative ties and enhancing information flow with our Federal, State, Tribal, and local partners through a variety of specialized downgraded products that can be shared across a much wider audience. Most recently, NCTC developed a new unclassified magazine, *Alliance,* which features counterterrorism articles from FBI, DHS, and NCTC, and serves our State, local, and Tribal customers.

Strategic Operational Planning.—NCTC is charged with conducting strategic operational planning for counterterrorism activities, integrating all instruments of National power, including diplomatic, financial, military, intelligence, homeland security, and law enforcement activities. In this role, NCTC looks beyond individual department and agency missions toward the development of a single unified counterterrorism effort across the Federal Government.

NCTC develops interagency counterterrorism plans to help translate high-level strategies and policy direction into coordinated department and agency activities to advance the President's objectives, for example in confronting ISIL and al-Qaeda. These plans address a variety of counterterrorism goals, including regional issues, the use of weapons of mass destruction by terrorists, and countering violent extremism. Additionally, working with our colleagues from DHS, FBI, and other agencies, NCTC engages with domestic and international partners on initiatives to improve resiliency, engage communities on countering violent extremism, and enhance response plans and capabilities in the face of evolving terrorist threats.

ADDRESSING THE THREAT FROM SYRIA FOREIGN FIGHTERS

NCTC draws on these capabilities and initiatives to address the threat posed by Syrian foreign fighters. The United States, the European Union—including the United Kingdom, France, and other member states—and the broader international community have increasingly expressed concerns about the greater than 15,000 foreign fighters who could potentially return to their home countries to participate in or support terrorist attacks. The United Kindom's Home Secretary announced the terrorist threat level in the United Kingdom had been raised to severe, explaining,

"The increase in threat level is related to developments in Syria and Iraq where terrorist groups are planning attacks against the West. Some of those plots are likely to involve foreign fighters who have traveled there from the UK and Europe to take part in those conflicts." This past week, Australia also raised its threat level from medium to high.

Syria remains the preeminent location for independent or al-Qaeda-aligned groups to recruit, train, and equip a growing number of violent extremists, some of whom we assess may seek to conduct external attacks. The rate of travelers into Syria exceeds the rate of travelers who went into Afghanistan/Pakistan, Iraq, Yemen, or Somalia at any point in the last 10 years.

European governments estimate that more than 2,000 Westerners have traveled to join the fight against the Assad regime, which include more than 500 from Great Britain, 700 from France, and 400 from Germany. Additionally, more than 100 U.S. persons from a variety of backgrounds and locations in the United States have traveled or attempted to travel to Syria.

NCTC, FBI, and DHS are part of a broader U.S. Government and international effort to resolve the identities of potential violent extremists and identify potential threats emanating from Syria. Central to this effort is TIDE, which is much more than a screening database—it is an analytic database. It feeds the Unclassified screening database so that DHS, the State Department, and other agencies have access to timely and accurate information about known and suspected terrorists. Initiatives such as Kingfisher aid in this screening process. As disparate pieces of information about KSTs are received, trained analysts create new records in TIDE, most often as the result of a nomination by a partner agency. The records are updated—or "enhanced"—regularly as new, related information is included and dated or as unnecessary information is removed. In all cases, there are several layers of review before a nomination is accepted into the system. In the case of U.S. persons, there are at least three layers of review, including a legal review, to ensure the derogatory information is sufficient and meets appropriate standards.

To better manage and update the identities of individuals who have travelled overseas to engage in violence in Syria and Iraq, we've created a special threat case in TIDE. This is a special feature in the TIDE system which allows us to focus efforts on smaller groups of individuals. A threat case links all known actors, and their personal information, involved in a particular threat stream or case and makes that information available to the intelligence, screening, and law enforcement communities.

NCTC's management of this unique consolidation of terrorist identities has created a valuable forum for identifying and sharing information about Syrian foreign fighters—including ISIL—with community partners. It has better integrated the community's efforts to identify, enhance, and expedite the nomination of Syrian foreign fighter records to the Terrorist Screening Database for placement in U.S. Government screening systems.

Counterterrorism efforts focused on law enforcement disruptions are critical to mitigating threats. We also recognize that Government alone cannot solve this problem and interdicting or arresting terrorists is not the full solution. Well-informed and well-equipped families, communities, and local institutions represent the best long-term defense against violent extremism.

To this end, we continue to refine and expand the preventive side of counterterrorism. Working with DHS, in the last year NCTC revamped the Community Awareness Briefing (CAB), a key tool we use to convey information to local communities and authorities on the terrorist recruitment threat. The CAB now also includes information on the recruitment efforts of violent extremist groups based in Syria and Iraq. Additionally, this year NCTC and DHS developed and implemented a new program—the Community Resilience Exercise program, designed to improve communication between law enforcement and communities and to share ideas on how to counter violent extremism.

CONCLUSION

Confronting these threats and working with resolve to prevent another terrorist attack remains the counterterrorism community's overriding mission. This year, NCTC celebrates its 10th year in service to the Nation, and we remain focused on continuing to enhance our ability to counter the terrorist threat in the years ahead.

Chairman McCaul, Ranking Member Thompson, and Members of the committee, thank you for the opportunity to testify before you this morning. I look forward to answering your questions.

Chairman MCCAUL. Thank you, director. I now recognize myself for questions. We mentioned there is no specific and credible threat to the homeland. But having said that, I don't think I have seen a threat environment any higher. Particularly as it exists overseas, with the spread of the so-called Islamic State in the Levant. We have known about this threat for over a year.

I don't think it was until the beheadings of the journalists, and now the British aid worker, that it really got the attention of the American people as to what kind of evil we are dealing with. It has changed popular opinion, in terms of driving policy to eliminate a threat that they don't want to see here in the United States, perpetrating those acts of brutal savagery.

At the same time, you have core al-Qaeda and Zawahiri in what appears to be a competition now with ISIS or ISIL to see who is the true heir apparent to bin Laden. It is a dangerous competition. The way I see it is to up the ante. What better way to do that than to attack the West? Coupled with 30,000 of these ISIS fighters, 15,000 are foreign fighters, over 100 American U.S. citizens. Many of these fighters have Western passports. So the ease of travel going back and forth obviously concerns homeland security officials and the intelligence community and the FBI.

So, first, I want to congratulate the FBI on the half a dozen or so arrests that have been made, including two in my backyard in Austin, of individuals traveling—wanting to travel to Syria or those who have—they have come back, who could have pulled off a terrorist attack, and you stopped that.

But at the same time, I am concerned about what you don't know what you don't know. I don't know what our level of confidence is in terms of who is on the ground, both in the United States and Syria that could imply a future attack in the United States.

So my question to the panel, and we have seen, you know, the Florida gentleman left Florida, went to Syria, came back, went back to Syria. It was a suicide bomber. We did see Tamerlan who was on the radar actually leave the United States and come back virtually undetected to pull off a terrorist attack. That is the kind of profile that I am concerned about and want to stop.

What assurances can you give this committee that we will be able to stop that type of foreign travel or foreign fighter from coming back in as a trained jihadist and killing Americans, Director Comey?

Mr. COMEY. Well, thank you Mr. Chairman.

It is something that the people at this table and the thousands of people we represent work on every single day to try to use our human sources, both here and abroad, and our technical resources to try and identify those who want to travel. Our first mission is to identify those and lock them up before they go. If they go, to try and keep very close tabs on them so that we know when they are headed back here so we can interdict them overseas. That is our preference. Or we can lock them up when they arrive.

Very difficult, as you alluded to. We have an enormous, wonderful, free country. There are thousands of ways to get from the United States to Syria, and there are tens of thousands of Americans who travel for legitimate purposes every single day.

So, sorting among that group to find the bad guys is something we spend every single day focused on. We have had good success, but I am not overconfident, given the nature of the challenge.

Chairman MCCAUL. Secretary Johnson.

Secretary JOHNSON. Chairman, the question of——

Chairman MCCAUL. Can you turn your mic up? Thank you.

Secretary JOHNSON. The question of our degree of confidence is one that the three of us talk about. My impression is from the information we know and the systems that we have in place to track those who travel, attempt to travel to Syria, is—from that, I think we have a reasonable degree of confidence, not a high degree of confidence, but a reasonable degree of confidence that we know the numbers, and we know who is attempting to travel.

The FBI has done a very good job of investigating, arresting, and prosecuting those who are attempting to leave the country, as you mentioned. There was another arrest just yesterday, and we are enhancing our ability to share information in the National security community of the U.S. Government and with our allies.

We are evaluating ways to potentially limit the travel of those who want to leave this country to go to Syria and pick up the fight. That is something we are in the midst of doing right now.

As I think you know, Chairman, we have been focused on the issue of foreign fighters for some period of months. In February, I said that Syria had become a matter of homeland security, principally because of this issue of foreign fighters. So, monitoring, interdicting the travel of those who might want to leave this country and go there is an area of top concern, right now.

Chairman MCCAUL. Well, I think you were the first one to say Syria poses the greatest threat to the homeland, and one of the first ones to say that, so I appreciate that.

Director Olsen.

Mr. OLSEN. Chairman, I would just add that you know, this is an effort that begins with good intelligence. So, the better intelligence we can get, particularly looking overseas, at who is traveling into Syria, who is seeking to leave Syria, the better position we will be to apply the various multiple layers of screening that are available to prevent those travelers from entering into the United States.

As my colleagues have said, we have been focused on this for many, many months. The area that I am encouraged by most recently is the level of attention that this is getting with our allies in Europe in particular, and how closely we have been able to work with them to share information and buttress their ability to interdict individuals seeking to travel to Syria or return from Syria.

Chairman MCCAUL. In my limited time, I do want to hit on the other threat, and that is within the homeland. This idea of homegrown, violent extremism. Radicalization from within. I know Pete King had many hearings on this topic last Congress.

There are two very glossy publications, one is—we have known about this one for awhile, *Inspire* magazine, which has come out with a recent edition. Page after page of how to make IED explosives, how to make bombs. Then this one from ISIS, a very glossy, in English—it is what I called when I wrote my *Wall Street Journal* op-ed, what they call jihad cool. This recruiting effort that they have on-going to train, to recruit, and radicalize Americans in the United States; not only to bring them to Syria, but also, God forbid, to pull off an act of terrorism in the United States. After all, they are already here.

I know the attorney general had a recent announcement on this. What can you tell me about that Mr. Secretary and Director, what the FBI and Homeland Security is doing to counter—and NTC, for that matter—counter this home-grown, violent extremist?

Secretary JOHNSON. Chairman, the Department of Homeland Security, for some time now, has had programs for outreach into communities in the United States that themselves have the capacity to reach those who might turn to violence.

We recently took that program and we put it into a separate office, which reports directly to the deputy secretary and me to enhance its visibility and enhance it as a priority. Our outreach people are all over the country in various different programs, and I have personally participated in these outreach programs.

I did one in suburban Chicago earlier this year with a Syrian-American community, and I am planning to do another one next week in Ohio. I agree with you that with the literature and the social media, and I have been through it myself, that heightens the risk of domestic-based extremism. Because people can learn tools of mass violence through literature, like what you just referenced.

So we have got our engagements. We are stepping it up. The attorney general announced earlier this week a pilot project focused on three cities, which we are all participating in, from DHS, the Department of Justice, FBI, and so this is a top priority, and we are very focused on it.

Chairman MCCAUL. Thank you. Director Comey.

Mr. COMEY. The only thing I would add to that is on the enforcement side, we are, the FBI, in every community in this country through our Joint Terrorism Task Force is working with our State and local partners to try to find these people and lock them up before they can actually harm somebody. So we are trying to make sure that we are touching communities of interest, that we are, in an on-line way, seeing what is going on, so we can spot folks, assess them, and then take them out of action if they really are a threat.

But as we have discussed, in a country this big and this free, with the material that is available, it is a big challenge for us.

Chairman MCCAUL. Thank you. They are very sophisticated in their social media. It makes it very difficult.

Just like Tamerlan, his postings were very radical, I know the FBI is getting very aggressive, trying to spot that kind of activity.

Director Olsen.

Mr. OLSEN. Just to add. I mean, a fundamental tenet of the strategy that we all work on together with respect to countering violent extremism is that the neighborhoods and communities that are at risk, they are in the best position to identify someone who is on the path to radicalization. So, an important part of this effort is to give them the tools, the education, the knowledge, the information to understand how magazines like the ones you just showed can influence an individual, and then be able to work with their

State and local law enforcement community and Federal law enforcement community to intervene when someone is on that path.

Chairman McCAUL. Thank you. Time has expired. I recognize the Ranking Member.

Mr. THOMPSON. Thank you, Mr. Chairman.

Secretary Johnson, there have been comments made relative to ISIL making attempts to enter from our Southern Border. Can you, for the sake of this committee, indicate whether or not there is any evidence that that has occurred or that anyone has been captured trying to enter our Southern Border?

Secretary JOHNSON. Congressman, we see no specific intelligence or evidence to suggest at present that ISIL is attempting to infiltrate this country through our Southern Border. I am sure my intelligence colleague could add to that.

Having said that, we do need to be vigilant. We do need to be aware of the risk of potential infiltration by ISIL or any other terrorist group. We have tools in place to monitor that and to do that.

Mr. THOMPSON. Thank you.

Mr. Olsen, you?

Mr. OLSEN. Yes, I agree with Secretary Johnson. There have been a very small number of sympathizers with ISIL who have posted messages on social media about this, but we have seen nothing to indicate that there is any sort of operational effort or plot to infiltrate or move operatives from ISIL through the—into the United States through the Southern Border.

Mr. THOMPSON. Thank you.

Director Comey, you talked about cybersecurity being upon your return, one of the new real threats. This committee has, on a very bipartisan basis, came together and has promoted what we think is one of the solutions to address many of the vulnerabilities that our cyber framework possesses.

Can you just enlighten the committee a little more on where you see some of those cyber threats coming from?

Mr. COMEY. Thank you, Mr. Thompson.

They come from everywhere. I call it a sort of an evil layer cake, with nation states at the top, terrorist groups, international criminal syndicates, hacktivists, and thugs and criminals and child abusers and pedophiles.

As I said, because our entire world is now on the internet, I am told soon my sneakers will talk to my refrigerator to tell the refrigerator I just went for a run.

But because our whole world is there, that is where those who would do us harm come. So, it runs every bad motive and every bad kind of person that you can imagine, that is where the threat is.

Mr. THOMPSON. Thank you.

Mr. Secretary, as you know, that legislation would have given DHS the resources and authorities that it needs to perfect and protect civilian networks and critical infrastructure. Do you see that type of legislation being important as we look at this vulnerability?

Secretary JOHNSON. Very much so, Congressman, and I appreciate and congratulate you and the Chairman and other Members of this committee for your leadership in this regard. I am aware that the bill that came out of this committee passed a full House, and I have spoken to your colleagues in the Senate about doing the same on the Senate side.

I believe it is critical. I have written an op-ed recently on the importance of cybersecurity legislation. There is real bipartisan support in the House and the Senate for cybersecurity legislation, and I think it is critical to our National security.

Mr. THOMPSON. Thank you.

Mr. Olsen, with respect to violent extremism, there—and to the extent that you can give information in this kind of setting—have you seen any difference in the recruitment and sophistication of ISIS or ISIL in comparison to other terrorist groups?

Mr. OLSEN. I would say that what we have seen from ISIL is a very sophisticated propaganda effort. The types of information that they are putting out on the internet, and in particular, using social media, really exceed the types of propaganda that we have seen from other groups. So, certainly, that effort has been quite sophisticated and extensive.

I think we still are—it remains to be seen the impact of that information on potential recruits. The one issue—one fact I could point to is, is the number of foreign fighters, and the significant number of foreign fighters that have traveled to Syria. Again, many of those—not all, but many of them joining ISIL's ranks. So, from that perspective, it is obviously a concern that the propaganda is having an impact in recruiting individuals.

Mr. THOMPSON. Last point is, with respect to violent extremism, and how we counter it, there is something you see our allies doing that maybe we should adopt as we look at how we as a country address that here?

Mr. OLSEN. We do work in coordination with our allies, particularly the United Kingdom, which has a strong program of countering violent extremism. We seek to learn from their lessons. They have had a little more experience with this than we have. So, our teams, both FBI and DHS and NCTC interact regularly with, in particular, our U.K. colleagues, to identify ways to improve our efforts in this regard.

Mr. THOMPSON. Thank you.

I yield back.

Chairman McCAUL. The Chairman recognizes the gentleman from New York, Mr. King.

Mr. KING. Thank you, Mr. Chairman. Let me thank you for holding this hearing. This is extremely timely and appropriate. Let me join you in welcoming the witnesses and thank Matt Olsen for his years of service. It has really been a—you know, a privilege to work with you, Matt. I want to thank you for what you have done.

Secretary Johnson, you have certainly hit the ground running, and I want to thank you for that. Also, for your visit to New York the other day. I think it is always important to remind the people even in New York about the constant terror threat that we face.

Director Comey, I think your being here today really does show the extensive cooperation that is needed among all of the counterterrorism forces in our country.

All of you have mentioned that it is not just ISIS, but it is also the whole panoply of al-Qaeda threats we have to face. AQAP, core al-Qaeda itself. You know, there is one group—and I am only mentioning this because it was in the media the last several weeks—the Korazon group. Is there anything you can tell us in an Unclassified setting regarding that?

If not, I understand. I am only mentioning it because it has been in the media.

Mr. COMEY. A discussion of specific organizations I think should be left to a Classified setting.

Mr. KING. I understand that.

Ranking Member Thompson asked a question about working with our allies. Director Comey, I would ask you, what are the pluses and minuses of Prime Minister Cameron's proposal that passports be taken away from people of particular countries that travel to Syria? So, in our case, Americans traveling to Syria—what are the pluses and minuses from your perspective—from the FBI's perspective—of taking away their passports?

Mr. COMEY. Thank you, Mr. King. That is a question I think probably better answered by Secretary Johnson. But just, quickly—it is of interest to us. I met with the home secretary, as I know Secretary Johnson did, from the United Kingdom this week, to try and understand better how that is working for them.

Among the concerns I would have is: What is the due process that would come with that in the United States? How would I protect sources and methods? How would we be able to use, if at all, Classified information to make the showing that would be necessary? So, I am interested in any tool that might help us identify and incapacitate these people. But I would want to understand the details a little bit better.

Mr. KING. Also, if I could ask, what would be the advantages of allowing them back into the country and monitoring them to see who they have contacted? Or is that too risky?

Mr. COMEY. No, we do it on a case-by-case basis in all manner of circumstances. Sometimes, it makes sense under limited circumstances to let somebody back in, cover them very closely to see who they connect with. Sometimes, it makes sense to have them come back in the country and lock them up right away. So, it is hard to say in the abstract.

Mr. KING. Secretary.

Secretary JOHNSON. I agree with the FBI director that the suspension of passports should be considered on a case-by-case basis. The State Department has the authority to suspend passports. I also know that suspension, revocation of passports can be done on an expedited basis when the situation warrants, in a matter of hours or days. It does not necessarily need to be a lengthy process. I agree, given the current environment, that we need to seriously consider limiting the ability of certain individuals to travel, either to go from one foreign country to another, or from our country to another country.

Mr. KING. Director Olsen. No?

I think this was touched on by the Chairman—how concerned are you of, let's say, to put it in simple terms, the rivalry between core al-Qaeda and ISIS, or AQAP and ISIS, as far as to get themselves back in the headlines or reestablish themselves as the No. 1 terrorist force, that they would—to increase the chances of an attack upon the homeland?

Secretary JOHNSON. I am very concerned about that. These groups are in competition with another for attention, for fund-raising, for recruitment. One way to compete is to show that you are the biggest and baddest group out there. So, I think that the environment we are in right now presents additional challenges. So, I agree with the premise in your question.

Mr. KING. Mr. Olsen.

Mr. OLSEN. I agree with Secretary Johnson. I think there is this concern about competition among these groups. One particular example of this would be the recent announcement by al-Qaeda core of a new affiliate in the Indian subcontinent. That was announced on social media on September 3. It could be viewed as an effort by core al-Qaeda to reassert its supremacy in this global movement.

So, those sorts of efforts can be viewed in the context of what might be an emerging competition among groups.

Mr. KING. Director Comey.

Mr. COMEY. You know, Mr. King, the logic of it is compelling because you are not going to be the leader in the global Jihad without striking America. So, it drives that sense of competition that my colleagues have talked about.

Mr. KING. Thank you all for your testimony.

I yield back. Thank you, Mr. Chairman.

Chairman MCCAUL. The Chairman recognizes Ms. Jackson Lee.

Ms. JACKSON LEE. I, too, would like to thank the Chairman and Ranking Member for this hearing. I would also like to thank each of the presenters—Members of the panel for your service to this Nation.

Having served on this committee from the beginnings of the recovery period of 9/11, when the Select Committee on Homeland Security was first formed to create this Department, I know how important the issues that all of you gentlemen are speaking of are to the Nation and to the security of America.

I think it is important even in this meeting to hold up the Constitution, to tell all of those who would have a malicious intent toward the United States is that we will not sacrifice our values, our liberty, our commitment to equality and justice for their terroristic ways. I thank all of you for recognizing, as my Ranking Member indicated, that we are not here to label a faith, Islam, or the Muslim people. We are here to ensure the security and safety of the United States of America.

I want to first of all say that as I was looking over materials that I think are relevant, I think it is important to note from an article, and I ask unanimous consent to put into the record an article by William McCants, who indicated that the issue or the idea of ISIL began in 2006, long before President Obama, long before Secretary Johnson or anyone was in the positions that they are in today, and before the American withdrawal from—and had at that time popular backing.

So let me be very clear. I believe our President has been very effective in trying to both downsize and bring down the war in Iraq and, as well, address the National security of the American people. I will not vote for an authorization for war, but we cannot talk about ISIL without doing something. So I will vote today for ensuring that other fighters, in this instance the Free Syrian Army, is well-trained to do the job. That means that we here in the United States must be very sure of what we are doing to protect the homeland.

Secretary Johnson, I would ask as a follow-up question on my colleague, Mr. Thompson. Coming from Texas, do you feel that you have sufficient Federal resources on the border to, if there was such an intrusion, that your staffing between ICE, which is on the inner side between the Border Patrol, intelligence, working with your colleagues, do you believe you have the right and necessary resources?

Secretary JOHNSON. We have more resources today than we have had at any time previously. Over the last several years, we have put at the border, particularly the Southwest Border, an unprecedented level of resources in terms of people, technology, vehicles, and other equipment.

As you know, I am sure, Congresswoman, apprehensions over the last 14 years have gone down. They have gone up this year because of the spike in the Rio Grande Valley sector. But we could use more. The bill passed by the Senate last year, S. 744, would have gone a long way to providing additional resources, additional personnel for the Southwest Border——

Ms. JACKSON LEE. Thank you.

Secretary JOHNSON [continuing]. Toward border security.

Ms. JACKSON LEE. Thank you.

Secretary JOHNSON. So——

Ms. JACKSON LEE. I wanted to be clear, if I could, because my time is running, that you do have—I do support that legislation and I would rather have the Federal resources than unpaid National Guard that has been put down by the Governor of the State of Texas.

Let me quickly ask a question to all of you. We know that we have been hacked. All of us have been hacked. But the question is, do you—are you able to discern the distinction between the identity-thief hackers and that of the state hackers that are coming in as terrorists on the cybersecurity grid? Could you all answer that question?

My last question, so I would get it in so you can answer, if you might. The women of this Nation are seemingly targets of recruitment for ISIL. Women coming from Western nations, poor, maybe uneducated—are we having a special target to recognize the concern for those women and how we would stop that? If all three of you could answer that, I would appreciate it.

Secretary JOHNSON. Congresswoman, let me begin with the question on cyber. As Director Comey suggested, we face cyber threats from a range of different types of actors. I think we do a pretty good job of detecting the nature and the type of actor for each specific attack, but it is a range from private individuals to others.

I will defer to my colleagues.

Mr. COMEY. I agree with Secretary Johnson, though attribution gets increasingly difficult as the private—the thieves get increasingly sophisticated and some of their techniques come to rival those of nation-states. But we do a reasonably good job of being able to sort them out.

With respect to the recruitment of women, you are absolutely right. There is a targeted effort by ISIL to attract fighters and people who would be spouses of fighters. Given the nature of their male orientation, the spouses are always women. They are trying to attract them from all over the West to come to their so-called caliphate to be—to start families in their warped world.

Ms. JACKSON LEE. Mr. Olsen.

Mr. OLSEN. I would only add to what Director Comey said about the recruitment of women. You know, among the most barbaric aspects of what ISIL has done in Iraq is the enslavement of women and young girls. So it is obviously a huge concern to us.

If I may add, Ms. Jackson Lee, you held up the Constitution, and today is Constitution Day.

Ms. JACKSON LEE. Yes, it is.

Mr. OLSEN. I would say that the director of National intelligence, Jim Clapper, yesterday held a swearing-in for those of us to reaffirm our commitment to the Constitution, with the workforce. I think that reflects the commitment within NCTC and the broader intelligence community to our fidelity to the Constitution.

Ms. JACKSON LEE. If I might, Mr. Chairman, thank Mr. Olsen for his service and ask unanimous consent—I believe I asked for unanimous consent for this—but I would also ask for unanimous consent, which I would like to refer to the Chairman's review, H.R. 5488, which I would like to ask unanimous consent just to put into the record, which is legislation that is called "No Fly For Foreign Fighters." It doesn't tie your hands, but it refines the watch list to make sure that everyone that should be on it is on it, particularly since the foreign fighter concept is continuing to grow.

I ask unanimous consent to introduce that into the record and look forward to discussing it with you gentlemen.

Chairman MCCAUL. Without objection, so ordered.

[The information follows:]

STATE OF CONFUSION: ISIS' STRATEGY AND HOW TO COUNTER IT

By: William McCants

Brookings, Foreign Affairs, Opinion/September 11, 2014
http://www.brookings.edu/research/opinions/2014/09/11-counter-isis-strategy-mccants

In 2005, Ayman al-Zawahiri, deputy head of al Qaeda, had a killer idea: the al Qaeda franchise in Iraq (AQI) should declare an Islamic state. In a letter to Abu Musab al-Zarqawi, the brutal leader of AQI, Zawahiri explained how it would work. The Islamic state, he wrote, would fill security vacuums around Iraq left by departing American forces. Once the Islamic state successfully fended off the attacks from neighboring countries that would undoubtedly follow, it could proclaim the reestablishment of the caliphate, the one-man institution that had ruled a vast empire in early Islamic history. For the scheme to succeed, Zawahiri warned Zarqawi, al Qaeda had to make sure that the Sunni masses supported the project.

Once it was loosed into the world, Zawahiri's idea was too powerful for him or the al Qaeda leadership to control. By 2006, long before the American withdrawal and far too early to have built up much popular backing, AQI had established Zawahiri's Islamic state. The new head of AQI after Zarqawi's death, Abu Ayyub al-Masri, dissolved his organization and pledged his allegiance to a new "commander of the faithful," Abu Omar al-Baghdadi, who purportedly controlled the Dawlat al Iraq al Islamiyya, or the Islamic State.

Baghdadi's title confused the jihadist community. In medieval Islam, "commander of the faithful" was usually reserved for the caliphs. Was Baghdadi claiming to be the caliph? And what of Mullah Omar, to whom al Qaeda's leaders had aleady pledged allegiance? The name of the group was also puzzling. The word for "state" in Arabic is dawla. Was the new group claiming to be a dawla in the modern sense, an institution jihadists believe is un-Islamic? Or was the Dawlat al Iraq al Islamiyya simply an ode to the name of the man revered as the greatest caliphate, the Dawla Abbasiyya?

The Islamic State was not eager to dispel the ambiguity. It either liked implying that it had more power than it actually possessed or believed that the jihadist community was not ready to tolerate the full freight of its claims. Ambiguous audacity captured the imagination and was thus the key to the group's power.

Although Zawahiri had first suggested the idea of establishing a state, he and the other al Qaeda leaders were blindsided by its early realization. Writing four years after the ISI was declared, Adam Gadahn, an American al Qaeda operative, confided in a private letter that "the decision to declare the State was taken without consultation from al'Qaida leadership," a move that "caused a split in the Mujahidin ranks and their supporters inside and outside Iraq."

Al Qaeda's official position, nevertheless, was to endorse the fait accompli, probably in an effort to keep a hand in the Iraq game and avoid further dissension in the ranks. "I want to clarify that there is nothing in Iraq by the name of al Qaeda," proclaimed Zawahiri in a December 2007 question-and-answer session. "Rather, the organization of [AQI] merged, by the grace of God, with other jihadi groups in the Islamic State of Iraq, may God protect it. It is a legitimate emirate established on a legitimate and sound method. It was established through consultation and won the oath of allegiance from most of the mujahids and tribes in Iraq." But neither point was true, as al Qaeda leaders privately groused.

Al Qaeda may have ratified its affiliate's decision to disband after the fact, but it was still an open question as to whether the Islamic State was subordinate to al Qaeda Central or an altogether independent entity. The state itself never addressed the question, again relying on ambiguity to imply greater power and independence than it actually possessed. And al Qaeda's leaders made the fateful decision never to dispel that uncertainty.

From private documents, though, we know that al Qaeda Central believed that the Islamic State was under its authority. In his private letter, for one, Gadahn claims as much. The United States also uncovered a paper trail of documents from 2007 and 2008 attesting to that fact. Al Qaeda Central ordered the Islamic State of Iraq to carry out attacks, for example, against Halliburton in 2007 and the Danes in 2008. Al Qaeda Central also asked for information on the state's personnel and expenditures. When the group refused to answer corruption charges leveled by one of its former officials, al Qaeda Central summoned Masri, the group's war minister and previously the head of AQI, to the woodshed in "Khorasan" (Afghanistan or Pakistan).

Whatever control al Qaeda exercised over the Islamic State of Iraq had further eroded by 2011, either because the Islamic State rarely heard from al Qaeda Central owing to U.S. counterterrorism measures or because the state did not want to listen to its superior. As Gadahn put it in his letter, "Operational relations between the leadership of al-Qaeda and the State have been cut off for quite some time."

Still, there was no formal break between the two organizations. Even Abu Muhammad al-Adnani, the Islamic State's spokesman, who today denies that the Islamic State of Iraq ever pledged an oath to obey al Qaeda, acknowledges that it was "loyal" to al Qaeda's commanders and addressed them as such, and that it continued to abide by al Qaeda's guidance on attacks outside Iraq. For example, he says, the group refrained from ever attacking Iran (even though its soldiers demanded it) out of deference to al Qaeda's desire to "protect its interests and its supply lines in Iran." The Islamic State also held back from carrying out attacks in Saudi Arabia, Egypt, Libya, and Tunisia because al Qaeda asked it to. But when it came to targeting decisions inside Iraq, the spokesman contends that it never followed al Qaeda's "repeated request" to stop targeting Shiites. And, in his telling, al Qaeda Central never issued a direct command or asked about the disposition of its forces inside Iraq. When al Qaeda's leaders expelled the group in 2014 for its disobedience, Adnani retorted that al Qaeda could not disown what had never belonged to it in the first place.

Adnani is lying, has a poor memory, or is unaware of high-level discussions between the Islamic State of Iraq and al Qaeda Central. Al Qaeda certainly inquired about the Islamic State's troops and issued requests and demands for it to change its targets, modify its tactics, and reform its bureaucracy, as the documents from 2007 and 2008 demonstrate. That al Qaeda usually couched its instructions in polite language does not mean al Qaeda expected the Islamic State to ignore them.

There are many reasons the Islamic State grew unruly, some of them bureaucratic—it is hard to govern a terrorist group remotely, especially when even the local leader loses control of a corrupt faction of the group—others security-related—

many of al Qaeda Central's messages were delayed or simply did not get through because of U.S. counterterrorism measures. But other al Qaeda affiliates bedeviled by the same infighting and hardships had never revolted. What separates them from the Islamic State of Iraq is also what explains its aberrant behavior: the group came to believe its own propaganda that it was, in fact, a state. Its flag—and not al Qaeda's—had become the symbol of the global jihad. Even al Qaeda's own affiliates flew it. Jihadist fanboys on-line counted the days since the state's establishment. And after the Islamic State began to control territory in 2012, it could truly claim to be a state in fact and not just in theory.

When, in 2013, the Islamic State (now calling itself the Islamic State of Iraq and al-Sham, or ISIS) proclaimed its authority over Syria and Iraq, Zawahiri demanded that it renounce that claim and return to Iraq. The response of the ISIS's emir was dismissive: "I have chosen the command of my Lord over the command in the message that contradicts it." Months later, ISIS proclaimed itself the caliphate, rallying many in the global jihadist community to its side. It is far more exciting to be fighting for a caliphate that has returned than for a distant promise of its return under al Qaeda. Zawahiri's killer idea had taken on a life of its own, dismembering al Qaeda and replacing it as leader of the global jihad.

Despite ISIS' success in capturing jihadists' imagination, the idea of an Islamic state has one fatal flaw: its physical incarnation makes it vulnerable to attack. Take away the state's territory and expose its brutality and rapaciousness, and you discredit the standard-bearer of the idea. You may even discredit the idea itself. As Adnani prayed in a recent message, if this state is false, then may God "break its back . . . and guide its soldiers to the truth." The United States and its allies should do everything they can to ensure that the higher power does indeed destroy the state—and expose the truth.

———

113TH CONGRESS
2D SESSION

H.R. 5488

To require a review of the completeness of the Terrorist Screening Database (TSDB) maintained by the Federal Bureau of Investigation and the derivative terrorist watchlist utilized by the Transportation Security Administration, and for other purposes.

IN THE HOUSE OF REPRESENTATIVES

September 16, 2014

Ms. JACKSON LEE introduced the following bill; which was referred to the Committee on the Judiciary

A BILL

To require a review of the completeness of the Terrorist Screening Database (TSDB) maintained by the Federal Bureau of Investigation and the derivative terrorist watchlist utilized by the Transportation Security Administration, and for other purposes.

Be it enacted by the Senate and House of Representatives of the United States of America in Congress assembled,

SECTION 1. SHORT TITLE.

This Act may be cited as the "No Fly for Foreign Fighters Act".

SEC. 2. REVIEW OF THE COMPLETENESS OF THE TERRORIST SCREENING DATABASE (TSDB) MAINTAINED BY THE FEDERAL BUREAU OF INVESTIGATION AND THE DERIVATIVE TERRORIST WATCHLIST UTILIZED BY THE TRANSPORTATION SECURITY ADMINISTRATION.

(a) IN GENERAL.—Not later than 90 days after the date of the enactment of this Act, the Attorney General, acting through the Director of the Terrorist Screening Center, shall complete a review, in coordination with appropriate representatives from the Department of Homeland Security and all other relevant Federal agencies, of the completeness of the Terrorist Screening Database (TSDB) and the terrorist watchlist utilized by the Administrator of the Transportation Security Administration to determine if an individual who may seek to board a United States-bound flight or a domestic flight and who poses a threat to aviation or national security or a threat of terrorism and who is known or suspected of being a member of a foreign terrorist organization is included in such Database and on such watchlist.

(b) REPORT.—Not later than ten days after the completion of the review under subsection (a), the Director of the Terrorist Screening Center shall submit to the Committee on Homeland Security of the House of Representatives and the Committee on Homeland Security and Governmental Affairs of the Senate a report on the findings of such review.

Ms. JACKSON LEE. Thank you very much. I yield back.

Chairman MCCAUL. Dr. Broun, from Georgia.

Mr. BROUN. Thank you, Mr. Chairman.

Director Olsen mentioned in his oral testimony that over, roughly—I am sorry—100 Americans have joined ISIL. Do we know how many Americans have actually joined ISIL, as well as other terrorist organizations around the world?

Any of you can give me a number?

Mr. OLSEN. I want to be very clear about the numbers, if I may, Congressman. So, we estimate over 100 Americans have traveled to Syria to join with extremist groups in Syria, or at least attempted to travel.

Mr. BROUN. So you don't know a number of who have actually joined, is that correct?

Mr. OLSEN. Once in Syria, it is very difficult to discern what happens there.

Mr. BROUN. Do you know who they are, though, that have joined or have traveled to Syria, have traveled to Pakistan or other places around the world? Do we know who those people actually are?

Mr. OLSEN. To varying degrees, we have specific information about who they are, whether they travel to Syria or other locations.

Mr. BROUN. Well, going back to what former Chairman Peter King was asking about passports. The State Department recently has said that they are not going to revoke passports on Americans that fly to Syria or fly to these different places. If we know who those people are, I think it is an outright security threat not to revoke their passports. Certainly, I believe in due process, but I think we can do this. It is a huge security threat to this country if we don't revoke their passports.

We already know that TSA has allowed known terrorists that are on the No-Fly List actually to get on aircraft in America. That presents a huge security threat to America.

Next question of all three of you is that we have got cities, and now the State of California, that have declared themselves as being sanctuaries for illegal entrants into this country. Do you all see this kind of philosophy of cities or even a State being a security risk to our Nation?

Mr. Secretary.

Secretary JOHNSON. I guess I would answer it this way. We have a pretty good ability through law enforcement, intelligence, homeland security means, to identify individuals, including undocumented, who are people of suspicion, suspected terrorists. The FBI proves that time and again.

I do think that in any situation where there are a large number of people who are undocumented, there is a risk that—it hinders our ability to track those individuals, which is why from my homeland security perspective, I would want to see those people come forward and get on the books so that I know who they are.

So, you know, if what you are suggesting is that the risk to homeland security grows when there are larger numbers of undocumented people in any one place, in any crowded area, I can't disagree with that.

Mr. BROUN. Well, we know that we have got a porous border, particularly on the Southwest. We already know that as your Department, Secretary, describes this, we have OTMs, other than Mexicans, crossing the border, that we have apprehended. We don't know how many people have not been apprehended. Would you agree with that statement? Yes or no.

Secretary JOHNSON. We generally believe that—we have an ability to calculate total attempts to cross the border illegally. Apprehensions are a large percentage of that. It runs somewhere between 70 and 90 percent. So we track total attempts. So we have a sense for who we didn't get who has crossed the border.

Mr. BROUN. Well, I have limited time. I apologize for interrupting you. Do we know how many Syrians or Pakis—Pakistanians or Iranians or Somalians or others have crossed the border?

Secretary JOHNSON. In a broad sense. There is obviously legal migration and there are obviously a large number of people who travel from those countries for legitimate means, through lawful means. So I think we have a pretty good sense of the nationalities of who comes to this country, both through legal migration and through apprehensions.

Mr. BROUN. Well, frankly, I believe that this Visa Waiver Program that we have increases our security threat, too, because of these terrorists being able to fly to this country with—on the Visa Waiver Program. I think we need to, Mr. Chairman, look at that.

One final question: Some Americans say that ISIL and what is going on in Syria and Iraq today are just involved in a local civil war. What would you all say to them as far as the threat that this poses to our own interests here in this country? If I could get all three of you to respond to that.

Secretary JOHNSON. I will start.

Congressman, I think that ISIL represents a huge threat to our interests. It represents a potential threat to our homeland security. It represents a threat to the stability in the region, and it obviously represents a threat to Americans in the region. They demonstrate the willingness to kill Americans because they are Americans.

As the Chairman and others have pointed out, they have acquired territory. We have to be very concerned any time any terrorist organization acquires territory for training, for launching attacks.We are determined to take the fight to this group.

Mr. BROUN. Director Comey, would you comment, please?

Mr. COMEY. I agree with what Secretary Johnson said. I wish it were the case that it was something that was in a box halfway around the world, but it is not.

Mr. BROUN. Okay.

Director Olsen.

Mr. OLSEN. I completely agree with Secretary Johnson and wound only add that there is certainly no lack of understanding within our departments and agencies or within the intelligence community of the nature of the threat that the group poses.

Mr. BROUN. Thank you so much. Mr. Chairman, my time has expired. I yield back.

Chairman MCCAUL. Gentleman's time has expired. Given the limited time we have with our witnesses, I am going to hold Members very strictly to the 5-minute rule.

Next we have Mr. Barber, who is not here, so Mr. Payne, who is also—where is Mr. Payne? He is right next to me. You changed seats with the Ranking Member.

[Laughter.]

Mr. PAYNE. Thank you, Mr. Chairman. Mr. Secretary, you know, recently there have been news reports that have claimed thousands of foreign students have overstayed their visas and have disappeared.

However, the Department of Homeland Security is doing a great job, and their own data appears to show that while these cases were initially flagged for review, the locations of these students was in fact known by DHS field officers.

It is my understanding that, you know, there are many reasons why a record might be flagged as a potential overstay, none of which are reasons to expect dangerous activity. For example, DHS's own press office has stated that many cases appear to be closed due to a variety of legal reasons, including the student's receipt of a green card or a departure from the United States.

You know, for generations American foreign policy leaders have agreed that educational exchanges are one of the most successful foreign policy tools. Eight of the Nobel Peace Prize winners since 1987 have been foreign students educated in the United States.

America needs friends and understanding around the world more than ever, and educating young people here gives us a great opportunity to develop those ties for future world leaders. Therefore, we need to understand how the Department manages the student visa program.

Can you discuss what the procedures and the systems DHS uses to monitor foreign students? Because I want to make sure that we do not distract the American people from the real threats that we are currently facing by mischaracterizing foreign students.

Secretary JOHNSON. Congressman, given the nature of student visas, we have to depend to a very large degree on what the universities tell us about whether the individual is still a student, still seeking an education in this country.

As you referenced, there have been a number of individuals who have overstayed their student visas. This is something I have looked into, taken a special interest in. I believe that there are a number of vulnerabilities in our ability to track these individuals that are being addressed.

A number of gaps are being closed. We have looked into the number of those who are reportedly overstaying their visas. We have found that a very large fraction have either been arrested or have returned to their countries or are in compliance to the receipt of green cards.

There is a fraction of that population where there are still open investigations. But, I don't have the exact numbers off-hand, but a very, very large number of those who were initially individuals of concern we have found either are now in compliance or have returned, but there are still open investigations on some.

So I think we are doing a better job of tracking these individuals. I totally agree with what you said about the importance of student visas and the importance of receiving an education.

Mr. PAYNE. Thank you. Because, you know, I just—I saw a report where they had used a number of 60,000, which absolutely was ridiculous and absurd. You know, it appears that the number is closer to maybe 6,000. But ICE has been on top of closing and narrowing that number consistently. Is that correct?

Secretary JOHNSON. That is correct. Of the 6,000 you referred to, we have found that a large number are either in compliance or have returned or have been arrested. There are still a number—I don't have the number off-hand, but there are still a number that is a fraction of that 6,000 that are under investigation. But I believe most of them are either in compliance, have been arrested or returned.

Mr. PAYNE. Okay. Thank you, and I will yield back.

Chairman MCCAUL. Gentleman from Pennsylvania, Mr. Meehan, is recognized.

Mr. MEEHAN. Thank you, Mr. Chairman. Director Comey, I appreciate your focus on the issue of technology. I enjoyed your anecdote about the fact that your sneakers may tell your refrigerator that you went for a run. I know you appreciate that those same sneakers could tell your wife that you went to the refrigerator.

But I do appreciate your leadership on the technology front, and I am struck by your concept that—your observation after 10 years returning, you are seeing the dramatic change and the metastasis as you identified it in the cyber domain. You know, we see the fifth dimension of warfare being in this cyber capacity.

One of our colleagues, former colleagues Lee Hamilton who observed this same phenomenon from our time together in 2001 came back and testified earlier in the week that he sees the cyber threat as even greater than the collective threat currently coming from ISIL.

So we know about the use of the radicalization and the recruitment that has been done. We have seen more sophisticated attacks from Iranians that have been tied to denial of services of our banks. We have seen criminal gangs use the internet for the creation of ways in which they can do things like extortion and to raise revenues.

I am also genuinely concerned about the ability to purchase expertise out there in the world-wide domain from people that may not be directly associated but can be hired to conduct activities. Of course there are some concerns that even at a certain point the kind of Islamic jihad could be tied back to ISIL with cyber attacks that look at Government organizations, energy companies, transport systems, banks, things of that nature.

In light of that, looking specifically at ISIL, what do you think the cyber dimension is of the cyber threat that ISIL creates?

Mr. COMEY. Thank you, Mr. Meehan. I remember fondly our time working together. Thank you for caring so much about these issues because I do think it transforms all of the things we are responsible for.

I see ISIL focused most on using the internet, cyber space, to recruit, both through sort-of peer-to-peer communications to try and lure people to come and fight for them, but also as the Chairman said, though their very slick propaganda efforts to energize and to train would-be fighters. I know this is something NCTC has spent a lot of time thinking about as well.

Mr. MEEHAN. Have you seen something, Mr. Olsen, with regard to the activities that lead you to believe that there is a growing competency that may create an actual threat from ISIL on the cyber domain?

Mr. OLSEN. It is something we are concerned about, but at this point I would characterize it as basically just aspirational in terms of any capability of ISIL or other similar groups to carry out cyber attacks. I think as Director Comey said, the primary concern about cyber right now is the use of the internet to recruit and attract followers.

Mr. MEEHAN. Okay. Director Johnson, you—or Secretary Johnson, you may feel comfortable in commenting on that, but I want to take my remaining minute to thank you for your leadership of and close cooperation with this committee as we have worked to structure new legislation that would enhance the ability for the agencies across the board to better prepare to be responsive to this growing technological threat and particular the use.

Can you tell me not just—I know you support it, but can you tell me why you believe this legislation is critical to the enhancement of your mission and why it is so critical that we act in a timely fashion on this?

Secretary JOHNSON. Congressman Meehan, thank you for your leadership in this area. I think it is critical. The reason—there are are several reasons why I believe legislation in this area is important.

One, to codify the authority of DHS to act in the dot-gov world. There is legal uncertainty about our ability to protect the dot-gov world. There are statutes that some would interpret to inhibit our ability to protect the dot-gov world. So the existing statutory landscape needs clarity in order for us to do our job.

We know also that in the private sector there are those who are concerned about their legal authority to share information with the Government. They are concerned about their civil liability—their potential civil liability if they share information with the Government, if they act in response to the Government.

We are also looking to enhance our authority to hire cyber talent. But one of my immediate concerns which I know you are focused on is clarity in terms of helping us police the dot-gov world. This is something we have got to do on a daily basis. We face attacks on a daily basis. It is not just a cybersecurity threat anymore.

Mr. MEEHAN. Well, I thank you again for your leadership, and particularly the promotion of the NCIC of the kind of junction through which a lot of this activity can take place and how vital it is.

Mr. Chairman, thank you for your leadership on that issue, and I yield back.

Chairman MCCAUL. Thanks for your leadership on cyber. Secretary, your strong support and the administration's support for passage in the Senate, and I—we all appreciate that as well.

Chairman recognizes Mr. Higgins.

Mr. HIGGINS. Thank you, Mr. Chairman.

Just first, on the ISA or ISIL numbers. You know, about 5 weeks ago in published reports, it was estimated to be between 7,000 and 11,000 ISA fighters. The most recent CIA report puts that estimate at 31,000. I am just wondering if that distinction is a result of bad numbers analysis or rapid recruitment success on the part of ISA?

Mr. OLSEN. Yes, Congressman.

So the current assessment is that their strength is anywhere between 20,000 and approximately 31,000—31,500. So it is—that obviously demonstrates that what we are talking about is an approximation with a large range. So we have limited intelligence on this question and that is by virtue of the fact that our ability to collect on this question is limited in Syria and in Iraq.

But the increase in that number does also reflect some of the recent gains that the group has made through its battlefield successes and its recruitment efforts, particularly in Iraq. So it is both. The change reflects our limited intelligence collection, but also the gains the group made more recently.

Mr. HIGGINS. Since the commencement of air strikes, have those numbers dropped? Have the increases been reduced? Because I think part of the military strategy there is to stop the ISIS momentum because that, more than anything else, is probably the most potent recruitment advantage that ISIS has.

Mr. OLSEN. What we have seen from an intelligence perspective certainly is that the air strikes have had an impact on the military momentum of ISIL. So it has had an impact on the battlefield. I think we are—it is too soon to tell how those strikes will affect the overall numbers of ISIL fighters or their ability to attract people to join the ranks.

Mr. HIGGINS. So the estimate of future recruitment, in terms of ISA members is open-ended and unknown?

Mr. OLSEN. Well, I think that is right. How it will look in a year or more from now is, at this point a question that we——

Mr. HIGGINS. Well, let me tell you why I ask that question. You know, it is hard to know that—where this is going, because nobody saw it coming. If we saw it coming, we potentially could have acted earlier to hold its progress. We know that, you know, 15,000 foreign fighters traveling to Syria, 2,000 of which are from Europe and the United States, you know, begins to bring this closer to home. You know, ISA is younger than al-Qaeda. It is more aggressive. It is more brutal. It is better at raising money. It is more technologically sophisticated. This poses a major problem.

You know my district alone, last year there was a terror plot to blow up a passenger train that was thwarted. It was going through Niagara Falls and two individuals were indicted and thought to have al-Qaeda affiliation. In 2003, six home-grown terrorists from the city of Lackawanna were convicted of providing material support to al-Qaeda after having traveled to Afghanistan and participated in al-Qaeda training camps.

Just yesterday in Rochester, New York about 50 miles from my district, a man was indicted for attempting to provide material support to ISA, attempting to kill U.S. soldiers and for possession of firearms and silencers.

So you know, I think it is—people shouldn't be alarmed, but I think that the growth of ISA, our inability to come—and we have a strategy that is not fool-proof. It depends on people who we have not demonstrated any confidence in before—the Free Syrian Army and all of the thousands of militias that make that up. This is a major concern.

I saw it in the Secretary's statement, you know, there were five things that the Department of Homeland Security is doing, including aviation safety and a number of other things and that is fine.

But I just think that the threat of ISA to the American homeland is much—it is more existential than we are willing to acknowledge. The idea, again, is not to alarm anybody, but to prepare for what is a very, very serious situation that is metastasizing in that part of the world. They are not going to stop in Eastern Syria or Northwestern Iraq. They have a goal and it is very specifically defined. The borders in that part of the world, these people have no appreciation for, historically, because they had nothing to do with it. They are looking to upend the entire Middle Eastern region and wanting to claim it for themselves.

I yield back.

Chairman McCAUL. The gentleman's time has expired.

Mr. Duncan is recognized.

Mr. DUNCAN. Thank you, Mr. Chairman, and thank you for the timeliness of this committee. I want to thank the gentleman, Mr. Higgins, for his comments as well. Thank you, gentlemen, for you service to our Nation. You have an immense challenge ahead of you. We all recognize that we support it where we can. Having a dialog about the threats, global threats to safety and security is very, very important, not only for lawmakers and policymakers, but also the American people. I want to comment about—Secretary Johnson, you mentioned the OTMS and whether we—that you use a broad spectrum. Whether it is broad or narrow, the fact is we have no idea who is in our country or what their intent is.

One side of the political spectrum really wants to paint a rosy picture that we have a secure border. But the fact is Americans realize that we don't. We also—I think Americans are counting on us in this arena to transcend politics and work to keep the bad elements out of our country, to work to keep another 9/11 from happening. They expect you guys to transcend politics and focus on keeping us safe.

I grew up in the Cold War. At that time, we were, as a Nation, tracking troop movements of the Soviets, tank placements, surface and sub-surface ships and where they may be across the country and across the globe. Now we are tracking individuals. Foreign fighters who may have left our country or Europe and traveled to Syria to fight Jihad who may have been radicalized, who may have the ability to travel back to their county and may have the ability to come here.

In June, I was in Brussels. Before we got to Brussels, a foreign fighter had traveled to Syria, was radicalized, made his way back through Turkey and Germany. Germany actually knew about this individual, failed to let the Belgians know. He went into Brussels and shot up a Jewish museum. At least three, if not four, individuals lost their lives. He tried to flee through France and was caught at a bus stop with the very weapons he used to commit the crime.

Germany knew, but failed to share that information. We are relying on information sharing as we try to track individuals—foreign fighters as they travel around the globe. It is an immense challenge. To go back to what I mentioned earlier. We talked earlier or heard earlier about the hundred or so Americans that have gone to fight with ISIS. But we also have Somali Americans who have traveled to fight with al-Shabaab. We have got Boko Haram, al-Qaeda, wherever they may be, in the Arabian Peninsula or other places. Don't take your eyes off of al-Qaeda as we focus on ISIS, because it is still a threat.

The thing that I want to question about this morning is a Classified—actually it is Unclassified now, internal memo from FBI. On June 13, the violent criminal threat section sent out a request for information regarding encroachment admission creep by other Federal law enforcement into traditional FBI lanes.

It goes on to talk about mission creep by Homeland Security investigations. It is an issue in an alarming number of field offices.

I appreciate the director of FBI saying that that is really not an issue, but what I want to point out is DHS was stood up in 2003 to recognize—or after recognizing the stove-piping of information, the walls, or barriers of sharing information between agencies that possibly could have thwarted the 9/11 hijackings.

I go back to the comments I made earlier about Germany failing to let Belgium know about a foreign fighter that traveled through their country, who ended up killing some folks at a Jewish museum. We cannot afford to have these type of turf wars between agencies charged with keeping us safe.

Director, how do you combat that? How do you keep that mission creep issue from being an issue? I would love to hear from Secretary Johnson on how he feels about that.

Mr. COMEY. Thank you, Mr. Duncan.

By talking about it constantly. That report made my head explode, and so I shared that head explosion with every leader in the FBI to let them know how I think about it, which is that the FBI does nothing alone. To be effective in protecting the American people across all our responsibilities, we need the kind of partnerships you see actually visually represented by the two of us sitting together. There is just no other way to do it.

The American taxpayer should have no patience for turf battles. I have got none.

Mr. DUNCAN. Director, I appreciate y'all's communication. I am concerned about communication where the rubber meets the road, and that is where the communication needs to happen. If you have got turf wars going on, I am afraid that information may not be shared appropriately.

Mr. COMEY. Yep, and that is what I meant by talking about it. I am pushing that. I have visited now 44 of my 56 field offices. I talk about it everywhere I go to make sure that I am shaping the culture in the right way, and I think that is an exception, that particular—what is reflected in that particular news account. I think we have made tremendous progress in 13 years, and we will keep working on it.

Mr. DUNCAN. That is his time. Thank you. Mr. Secretary.

Secretary JOHNSON. Congressman. Just yesterday, Director Comey and I got together to talk about cybersecurity to ensure that our organizations are working together effectively on cybersecurity. We both have a role in cybersecurity, along with other agencies. So, one of our challenges is to make sure that what you refer to doesn't happen, because that doesn't do any good for the American people, for our Government, for the taxpayers, to see us engaged in turf war.

So, we have committed to setting the example at the top and instilling that example in the rank-and-file in our leadership. So, on cybersecurity for example, we get together routinely to talk about what is our framework? Are we getting it right? Are we having any turf battles?

So, all three of us, I think, and I think I speak for our respective organizations and our respective communities, are committed to working together. I think it does depend a lot on the personalities at the top committing to work together.

The last thing I will say is your comment about DHS. In the 9 months I have been in office, I have seen the advantage of having the components within my Department together at one conference table. When we were dealing with the situation in the Southwest Border this summer in the Rio Grande Valley, I could put together at my conference table CBP, ICE, CIS, FEMA, and the Coast Guard to deal with the situation, to tell them what needs to be done.

These are entities that were scattered across the Federal Government, previous to the creation of DHS. So, I have seen the synergies of putting a lot of these components together in one Department. So, if that was the thrust of your comment, I very much endorse it and agree with it.

Mr. DUNCAN. Well, that was the whole idea. I am glad it is working. I am glad you are communicating with all your elements. That is why it was stood up. We need to learn from the 9/11 Commission Report. The reason we combated the stovepiping, the sharing of information, Americans are counting on you guys.

So, thank you so much, and God bless you.

I yield back.

Chairman MCCAUL. Thank you sir.

Chairman recognizes Mr. O'Rourke.

Mr. O'ROURKE. Thank you Mr. Chairman, for holding this hearing. I join my colleagues who said earlier that there is perhaps no way that the American public can know everything that each of you and the men and women who work with you have done to protect this country. Nonetheless, we owe you our thanks, and I want to join my colleagues in letting you know how much we appreciate it.

Secretary Johnson, I appreciate you setting the record straight on terrorist threats to the homeland from our border with Mexico. I could not agree more with you that despite our success thus far, that there have not been any terrorist plots connected to the Southern Border, that there is no evidence that ISIS is preparing to infiltrate the United States through the Southern Border.

I couldn't agree more with you that this is something that we need to remain vigilant against, and continue to guard against. Continue to use all of our resources as warranted by the threat that exists based on the evidence that we find.

I also appreciate you answering my colleague's question about whether or not we have sufficient resources on the Southern Border. We are spending $18 billion a year. We have 20,000 Border Patrol Agents, the vast majority of whom are on the Southern Border today. Those are double the numbers, more than double the numbers that we saw 5 or 6 or 7 years ago.

As you mentioned, the number of apprehensions is at a record low level. We saw 1.6 million apprehensions 15 years ago on the eve of 9/11, this year with the spike in Rio Grande Valley, I think it is going to be right at about half a million at the highest.

In the El Paso sector, the community I represent, the average agent apprehended 4.2 migrants or crossers this last year; 4.2 per agent. Now, that number does not reflect the deterrent value that those agents have. I think there is a lot to be said for that.

But you also said earlier that while we have sufficient Federal resources there, we could use more. You mentioned the Senate proposal, which I think was to add another 20,000 agents on the border. I am really concerned that when we know that the greatest risk is at our airports, we have talked about home-grown terrorists, that we are obsessively focusing on the Southern Border.

Again, let's remain vigilant, but we have finite resources. We should apply them where we have the greatest threats based on established risks that we have been able to determine. I would love to get your thoughts on that comment.

Secretary JOHNSON. Most people would endorse the notion of a risk-based strategy to homeland security, border security, aviation security. We focus resources where we believe the risk exists. It is an effective, efficient use of taxpayer dollars.

In aviation security, for example, we made the judgment to develop the TSA Pre-Check program, where we focus resources on the population we know less about. The Border Patrol experts that I have talked to also endorse that approach.

So, with additional personnel, additional boots on the ground on the border comes surveillance technology, the ability to monitor what is going on on the Southwest Border, to know where the threat areas are. Because they do migrate. They do move around.

We had a challenge this summer in south Texas.

So, I continually, with our Border Patrol personnel, look at where are the threat areas, how has it evolved, and so in my judgment, in response to your question, I think that a risk-based strategy is appropriate, and I think that technology, more technology, more surveillance, is the key to our future for border security.

Mr. O'ROURKE. Just following on your comments, my colleague sought analogy in previous conflicts to apply to this threat from terrorists who might want to enter the homeland. I also think about the French on the eve of World War II and their obsession with the Maginot Line. Yet somehow, through fortifications and a line of defense and a specific place, we are going to somehow solve a threat posed to this country.

I think we have to be far more creative and really be rigorous and disciplined about applying resources to where those threats are or where they could be based on established risk.

Last question to you, Mr. Secretary. There is a Southern Border and approaches campaign plan through DHS. Some have compared this to a SOUTHCOM type effort of organizing resources and assets against a specific threat. Could you very briefly describe the intent of that campaign, and where you are in its implementation?

Secretary JOHNSON. Well, first of all, going back to your previous question, I think I speak for my colleagues when I say none of us downplay or underestimate the risk of, or the concern of a terrorist or terrorist organization infiltrating our homeland. I mean, that is probably our primary concern, day-to-day, when we go to work every day, and it is something we have to continually be vigilant about.

The southern campaign plan is in development. I expect to be in a position to announce some things in the month of October concerning the southern campaign plan. It is an effort to more strategically bring to bear all of the resources of my Department on border security in a way that is not stovepiped, in a way that is strategic in how we use all our different resources within the Department.

Mr. O'ROURKE. Thank you.

Thank you, Mr. Chairman.

Chairman MCCAUL. The Chairman now recognizes Mr. Chaffetz.

Mr. CHAFFETZ. Thank you Chairman, and I thank all three of you for your dedication, for the men and women who serve in your departments and agencies.

Secretary Johnson, I want to thank you particularly for the good work the men and women are doing in Homeland Security. I can tell you, since you have taken office, the production and the response to Congress in terms of responding to our letters and inquiries is—the difference, I cannot tell you how much better it is. I thank you and the people who work on this. I do appreciate it.

Secretary JOHNSON. You may not like the responses, but you are getting them faster.

Mr. CHAFFETZ. Thank you. Yes. True.

Since you took office, Secretary Johnson, on December 23—or Secretary Johnson, on December 23, are you aware of any apprehensions of suspected or known terrorists who were trying to come to our country illegally?

Secretary JOHNSON. That is an important question. Attempting to come to this country?

Mr. CHAFFETZ. Who came across our border illegally. Did you ever apprehend anybody who was a known terrorist, a suspected terrorist, somebody who had ties to a terrorist organization?

Secretary JOHNSON. Sitting here right now, no specific case come to mind. That doesn't mean there is none. Perhaps Director Comey can think of one. Sitting here right now, I—none comes to mind, but that doesn't mean there isn't one, nor does that mean there is no investigation of one either.

Mr. CHAFFETZ. My concern is that I have a reason to believe that on September 10, there were actually four individuals trying to cross the Texas border who were apprehended at two different stations, that do have ties to known terrorist organizations in the Middle East.

Were you not aware of that?

Secretary JOHNSON. I have heard reports to that effect. I don't know the accuracy of the reports or how much credence to give them. But I have heard reports to that effect.

Mr. CHAFFETZ. I guess that is my concern, is you, as the Secretary, does that information rise to the level of the Secretary? Let me give you some metrics and some of the reason I am concerned about what is going on on the Southwest Border. This is an internal document of yours. While there were, as noted, nearly 466,000 apprehensions over the last 351 days, we also had 157,012 gotaways; we had 142,630 reported turn-backs.

But one of the other metrics that is also fascinating to me is the sensors that are found there primarily throughout the Southwest. We had just under 5 million sensor hits in fiscal year 2013. But in fiscal year 2014, over the last 351 days, we have now had more than 6 million of those hits.

Now, we have got wild burros and tortoises and animals that—there are a lot of false positives there. But the concern is if you look at the apprehensions, we have apprehended people from 143 different countries—143 countries, according to the internal statistics; 13 were from Syria; six were from Iraq; four were from Iran. The list goes on to 143 different countries.

The men and women that work on our Southwest Border, they do an amazing job. But to suggest that we have operational control of the border, I—help me understand this. You said there was a 70 to 90 percent success rate. Explain to me what that is.

Secretary JOHNSON. When you look at what we believe to be total attempts to cross the border illegally, the estimated rate of those who make the attempt, of those who are apprehended, is somewhere between 70 and 90 percent. It varies in time and it varies in sector.

Mr. CHAFFETZ. Now, the GAO—previously, the GAO had indicated that there was only a 6 percent operational control of the border. What percentage—what is the operational control of the border at this time?

Secretary JOHNSON. I don't have that number off-hand. I do agree with you that the challenge of those coming from countries other than Mexico, particularly into the Rio Grande Valley sector, is one I am very concerned about. It is something that I have been concerned about since I took office in January. I have seen it myself at our detention center in Brownsville when I visited there in January. There was something like 80 nationalities of illegal migrants present there.

Mr. CHAFFETZ. I need to interrupt because I have just a little time. I have got to switch real quick to a yes or no question.

In 1983, President Reagan put in place a prohibition on Libyan nationals from seeking visas to come to the United States to be trained in aviation security—or aviation and nuclear sciences. Myself, the Judiciary Chairman Bob Goodlatte, Congressman Trey Gowdy, and I introduced a piece of legislation that would keep that prohibition in place. There has been a process going through—through your offices and through the administration to actually reverse that prohibition that was put in place in 1983. That now sits on your desk. What is your view of lifting that prohibition?

Secretary JOHNSON. I do not intend to lift that prohibition at this time. I don't believe legislation to prevent me from lifting it is necessary. I think given the current environment, I do not intend to lift it at this time.

Mr. CHAFFETZ. I appreciate it. Thank you.

I yield back. Thank you.

Chairman MCCAUL. The Chairman recognizes Mr. Swalwell.

Mr. SWALWELL. I thank the Chairman. To our witnesses, 13 years ago I was a Congressional intern here in this town when September 11 happened. I watched with great interest our country's response to September 11 and I watched the creation, Mr. Secretary, of your Department and this committee become a full standing committee.

Now I think what we are experiencing with the rise and spread of ISIL in the Middle East and our efforts to respond to it is exactly why this Department was created.

So first, I just want to thank you, Mr. Secretary, and the two directors for the work you do every day to answer to these challenges to keep us safe here at home. Because while we are going to consider today what offensive measures we may take abroad, the critical component that I am most concerned about is what are we doing here at home.

So first, I just want to get out of the way something that my college from Texas alluded to. Mr. Secretary, do we have any evidence of any of the following groups coming across our Southern Border: ISIL?

Secretary JOHNSON. We have no specific intelligence that members of ISIL are crossing into the United States on our Southern Border.

Mr. SWALWELL. How about Hezbollah?

Secretary JOHNSON. Director Olsen could comment more specifically, or correct me on that, but——

Mr. SWALWELL. I will just go one by one, and if you think it takes further elaboration. How about Hezbollah? Yes or no.

Secretary JOHNSON. Same answer.

Mr. SWALWELL. How about al-Nusra?

Secretary JOHNSON. I believe the answer is the same. But again, I want to defer to my intelligence community colleague here in terms of any assessments of the current environment.

Mr. SWALWELL. May I also ask, in addition to not stopping anyone or interacting with anyone or interdicting anyone who is coming across who is not a member of these groups, would it also be safe to say that the intelligence community has not collected any information in the various means and methods it uses to collect intelligence, that there are efforts underway to use the Southern Border to go into the United States?

Mr. OLSEN. I think that is true certainly with respect to your first question, Congressman, on ISIL. We have seen, as I mentioned, chatter on, from sympathizers about that question, but we have seen nothing to indicate any efforts to enter the border—enter the United States through the Southwest Border by ISIL.

Mr. SWALWELL. I was in Jordan, Egypt, Morocco, and Israel 2 weeks ago and met with our State Department teams and our allies over there. My greater fear is not the Southern Border, but we were told about the number of Americans who are over in Syria and Iraq fighting shoulder-to-shoulder with ISIL, as well as the number of Westerners who are over there.

I was hoping that you could elaborate on what we are going to do or what we are doing to disrupt any plans of theirs to return to the United States and carry out with the tools and hate that they have built and developed abroad?

Secretary JOHNSON. Congressman, we have made enhanced efforts to track these individuals within the various communities of the U.S. Government. As you heard me mention, we have enhanced our aviation security measures. We are making enhanced efforts. We have stepped up our dialogue with our allies, with our partners there.

The President will chair a U.N. Security Council session next week on the topic of foreign fighters. We are considering a number of things to do that will give us more information from passengers from the countries, from visa waiver countries so that we know more about individuals who attempt to travel.

There is always law enforcement. I believe the FBI does a terrific job from the law enforcement perspective of investigating and arresting people who attempt to join terrorist organizations, who attempt to leave the country. I believe our allies also understand the nature of this threat and are making enhanced efforts as well.

Mr. SWALWELL. With the number of foreign fighters coming into Syria and Iraq, I have asked that you, Mr. Secretary, and others from the Department, that we really expedite the number of visa waiver countries who are participating in Interpol's Stolen and Lost Travel Documents Database.

Because I still remain concerned after what happened back in the spring with the Malaysian Airline's disappearance of two passengers who had boarded that flight with lost or stolen passports. I think now more than ever we need to make sure that we know and have these other countries really step up their efforts to report to Interpol. I—if you could just update us briefly on what we are doing to get these countries——

Secretary JOHNSON. We have been having that dialogue with our allies. I think they understand the nature of that issue.

Mr. SWALWELL. Great. Thank you again to each of you for what you are doing to keep us safe.

I yield back.

Chairman MCCAUL. Let me say, this committee is considering legislation to require visa waiver countries to provide more data and information in exchange for that privilege.

So with that, the Chairman now recognizes Mr. Barletta.

Mr. BARLETTA. Thank you, Mr. Chairman.

I don't know if we are making the argument here of whether or not we should secure our Southern Border or not. That is the feeling I am getting. There has been a lot of talk that if any terrorists—whether or not any terrorists have crossed the border illegally. But we do know that those wishing to do us harm have manipulated in the past our immigration system to enter and remain in the United States.

Mahmoud Abouhalima, he was a convicted perpetrator of the 1993 World Trade Center bombing; received amnesty in 1986 after he claimed to be an agricultural worker, despite being a cab driver in New York. The only thing he planted in America was a bomb.

President Obama has told the American people and potential terrorists that he plans to grant some form of administrative amnesty to potentially millions of those currently in the country unlawfully.

Secretary Johnson, as you make recommendations to the President as to how he should implement such a program, how will you assure the American people that another Abouhalima will not slip through the cracks?

Secretary JOHNSON. Congressman, I am very focused on knowing as much as we can about individuals who are undocumented in this country. I believe that—if an earned path to citizenship would have become law, that would encourage people to come forward and submit to a background check, so that they can get on the books. I know there is a lot of debate about—just give me a second, please—there is a lot of debate about the earned path to citizenship. From my homeland security perspective, I want people who are living in this country undocumented to come forward and get on the books and subject themselves to a background check, so that I can know who they are. Whether it is the current DACA program or an earned path to citizenship, whether it is deferred action or an earned path to citizenship, from my homeland security perspective, I want people to come forward and submit——

Mr. BARLETTA. But Secretary Johnson, I have dealt with this as a mayor in my hometown. Do we honestly believe that any would-be terrorists or a criminal or a drug dealer, is going to come forward to have a criminal background check done on them or are they going to continue to remain underground? Nobody with a criminal record is going to come forward.

Secretary JOHNSON. The more I can learn about the undocumented population in this country, the better; the more effectively we can use our removal resources against the type of person you just described, the better. So, I am interested in going after public safety National security threats in terms of our removal resources. I want to have a system that more effectively gets to that population——

Mr. BARLETTA. Do you believe Mahmoud Abouhalima would have come forward for a criminal background check in 1993?

Secretary JOHNSON. Most criminals do not subject themselves to criminal background checks; I agree with that.

Mr. BARLETTA. So he still would have planted that bomb in the World Trade Center. So the 9/11 Commission Report that I have here, I question why—this was a report and recommendations that was passed by Congress and signed by the President—why we haven't taken those recommendations and enforced them. The summary in the very first line, it says enforcement of our immigration law is a core component that, according to the Commission, up to 15 of the 19 hijackers on September 11, could have been intercepted or deported through more diligent enforcement of immigration laws.

Why are we not taking up the recommendations of the 9/11 Commission Report, so that we don't have another attack again?

Secretary JOHNSON. There are a number of 9/11 Commission recommendations that I wish we could all adopt.

Mr. BARLETTA. But enforcing our immigration laws is No. 1.

Secretary JOHNSON. Very plainly, enforcement of our immigration laws is a top priority of mine. With the resources that Congress gives us, we can and we should do an effective job of going after those who represent threats to public safety.

Mr. BARLETTA. Secure the borders.

Secretary JOHNSON. Secure the borders.

Mr. BARLETTA. The discussion here and we have had in the past in another hearing——

Secretary JOHNSON. I agree with you.

Mr. BARLETTA [continuing]. Whether or not——

Secretary JOHNSON. Securing the borders is——

Mr. BARLETTA [continuing]. Somebody has crossed the border already that is a terrorist. Nobody used a plane to crash into one of our buildings before, until the first time as well. That is not a good reason that we shouldn't secure the border, because we believe that nobody has crossed the border who is a terrorist already.

Chairman McCAUL. Thank you.

The Chairman recognizes Mr. Keating.

Mr. KEATING. Thank you, Mr. Chairman. I want to thank all three of our witnesses for their service, particularly Director Olsen, as you leave, for your service. It is pretty clear—also I want to thank, particularly Director Comey for being here for the first time. I appreciate it and I think it is very important.

It is clear from all your testimony that the No. 1 threat remains home-grown, radicalized, terrorists in our country. That is something that I think is heightened with the ISIL threat as well. There is a person that is on the Most Wanted list by the FBI as a terrorist, Ahmad Abousamra, who went to school, the same schools that one of my children did and then later went to school just a few miles away from them. It is close to home.

When you look at these threats and you look at the different challenges, I am reminded of our work that we did with the Boston Marathon bombing and that investigation that concluded that information sharing with local police is so important. Given Director Olsen's testimony about how ISIL has now become more sophisticated, it is harder to intercept messaging, that remains even more of a priority.

So, I would like to ask Director Comey to share with the committee the progress that you made in terms of doing a better job, sharing information with local police and also what progress is made in terms of formalizing that, too, in terms of a memorandum of understanding that can be there and transcend different administrations and the need, if any, for regulation of statutory change in that regard.

Mr. COMEY. Thank you, Mr. Keating. Yes, for anyone who was asleep before 9/11 and woke up today would not recognize the depth and extent of information sharing among Federal agencies and with our State and local partners; the world is transformed in that respect. But I also believe we can always find room to improve it. So a number of things we have done since Boston that I think have improved it is we have made clear that we want the default to be information sharing, and we don't want anything to be an impediment to that or misunderstood as an impediment to that.

We have also done something else that I think makes great sense, which is each of our Joint Terrorism Task Forces now has a regular meeting with all the leadership of the agencies involved to review our inventory—what came in over the last—it has to be with at least 30 days—30 days or a week or 2 weeks—what came in, what got closed, questions, concerns, to make sure everybody is in synch on what is going on in the JTTF.

There are a number of other smaller ways in which we—I think we have improved our information sharing. I travel around the country and meet with State and local law enforcement now in 44 field offices, and I am hearing good things. I think we are in a good place. But I don't want to rest on that, because there is always something I haven't thought of us, so I want to continue that dialog to improve it.

Mr. KEATING. I appreciate that. One of the areas that I have found that local officials aren't taking enough advantage of—local police now have access to Classified information more than they did. But it is my understanding they are not taking advantage of that the way they can. Is there something that we can do to help those numbers, to make it easier for them or to encourage them to get more of that information?

Mr. COMEY. I don't know, other than just encouraging it. I am urging all leadership of agencies to participate in our task forces, to at least get the Secret-level clearance. So that if you need to, you can see things very, very quickly. We are getting there. People are coming around to it. People are very, very busy. They also know that there are officers and detectives that are on our task forces, are cleared and are seeing everything. So I think that removes some of the sense of urgency, which I get, but we would like to encourage it more and more.

Mr. KEATING. I just want to follow up, too, that—I want to thank you for your meeting with me and your—our shared interest in information sharing with local and State officials.

I just wanted to reinforce the fact that, even though you are—I think you are the only seventh director, there will be a time that all of go from our different positions. It is the importance of having things in writing, whether is a memorandum of understanding or something that transcends that administration. What progress are we making in terms of having something in writing in that regard, in terms of information sharing?

Mr. COMEY. I think that makes good sense. Yes, I will—in 8 years and 51 weeks, I will be leaving this job. I would like to make sure that it doesn't depend upon people, but that the processes are documented.

Mr. KEATING. All right, thank you. I think Director Olsen wanted to talk.

Mr. OLSEN. If I could just add very briefly, Congressman, to Director Comey's answer to your question about Unclassified—or Classified information in State and local. Together, with the FBI and DHS, we have a program called the Joint Counterterrorism Assessment Team, in which we bring State and local police officers and firefighters to the National Counterterrorism Center, where they have access to all the most Classified information on a basis of detail more than 2 years.

They then help us design products that are Classified and turn those into Unclassified products. Again, working through DHS and FBI and their channels of communication with those communities, so that we can get what we are seeing at the Classified National level and turn it into information that is usable by police officers on the street and firefighters around the country. It has been a very successful program over the last several years.

Mr. KEATING. Great. I believe that is our first line of defense. I want to appreciate your efforts at making that easier to get.

I yield back, Mr. Chairman.

Chairman MCCAUL. I thank the gentleman.

The Chairman recognizes Mr. Perry.

Mr. PERRY. Thanks, Mr. Chairman.

Gentlemen, thank you very much for your service to the Nation. You have a very difficult job. It is a privilege to be here with you today.

Within—any of my questions, all of my questions, I would hope you would answer. Certainly, I know you would, but I want to acknowledge that I recognize the confines of operational security. But still, within whatever ability you can to answer the questions—Mr. Secretary, what are the Department's mechanisms in place that would prevent known American and European citizens fighting for terrorist organizations in Syria and Iraq from re-entering or entering the homeland?

Secretary JOHNSON. First of all, Congressman, we have our No-Fly List. That is the first thing that comes to mind.

Second, general aviation security. Though, unless you are carrying something suspicious, aviation security in and of itself wouldn't necessarily pick you up.

Passenger travel data, API data, PNR data. The more I can learn about travelers, the better. We have a fair amount. I think we can do a little better.

From visa waiver countries, passengers are required to answer questions on Electronic System for Travel Authorization called ESTA. We have as a condition for participation in the Visa Waiver Program security assurances that each Nation is required under what we call HSPD–6, which requires security assurances from visa waiver countries.

We have general information sharing with the National security intelligence community, communities within each of these other governments. So, with the current threat stream, the current environment, I think we all agree that we need to be particularly focused, particularly engaged in making sure that these mechanisms work appropriately.

Mr. PERRY. So, let me ask you this—I am not a—you know, was never in law enforcement, so I defer to you folks. But what I hear, it seems like—somewhat passive. I don't mean to degrade its ability and capability, but it seems somewhat passive. You know, asking a passenger to disclose information that is vital to us in securing the Nation, when their motives might be otherwise, seems less than optimal. So, I am looking to see if there is anything that we have done that is new, so to speak, that you would be, and should be willing to—or could be willing to divulge. Maybe anything that you might think that we should be looking at to get to the issue.

Secretary JOHNSON. Well, I want to defer to Director Olsen on this, but we can just outright prevent them from traveling——

Mr. PERRY. Right.

Secretary JOHNSON [continuing]. Or prevent them from entering——

Mr. PERRY. True.

Secretary JOHNSON [continuing]. The country. Or if they don't quite rise to the level of being on a No-Fly List, they should be subjected to some form of secondary screening, though—which is more than just answering questions. It gives us an opportunity to provide enhanced scrutiny on an individual before they get on an airplane. But Director Olsen, go ahead.

Mr. OLSEN. I think, exactly as Secretary Johnson said, there are a number of opportunities and layers of screening that occur for anyone trying to travel to the United States that—arriving at the border is just one point in time, but before they ever arrive here, one of the—there are opportunities to do that. One of the changes from the 9/11 Commission 13 years ago was to create a single consolidated database of known suspected terrorists. Together with the FBI and DHS and a number of other agencies, we have a single database that is consolidated across the Government of every known suspected terrorist that we have information about. That information, Classified, is then turned into an Unclassified watch list that is shared with the Terrorist Screening Center and a number of other agencies that have a screening responsibility. So, the No-Fly List is just one example.

But everyone who applies for a visa and everyone who seeks to travel here from a visa waiver country through the ESTA program—their information is screened against in that database. So, when they put their name and passport number into the system, whether they are applying for a visa or coming from a non-visa-requiring country, that information is then checked to see if they are on the watch list. They are either then subject to additional screening, or stopped altogether from traveling to the country.

Mr. PERRY. All right. I understand. I appreciate the answer. I am not here to be critical, so I am not going to be. I am just curious. While my—before my time expires—suspected ISIS social media accounts have called for unspecified border operations, where they have sought to raise awareness for illegal entry through Mexico as a viable option. Based on even some of your testimony that says that we have weak immigration laws, and the fact that we would use DACA, do you think that we should be concerned that they would use this propaganda to breach the Southern Border and use that as an operational tool? Should we, as Americans, be concerned about that possibility, based on everything that you know in our posture today?

Mr. OLSEN. Yes, absolutely, we need to be concerned about all the ways in which someone can enter this country for the purpose of carrying out a terrorist attack. As Secretary Johnson said, it is our overriding No. 1 priority, is to prevent that from happening.

Again, we need to be—we need to allocate our resources based on the information we have and where we see the threat. At this point, while we have seen some social media, I think in small numbers, not individuals who are sympathetic to ISIL, talking about the Southwest Border. We have seen nothing to indicate that there is actually any real effort to use the Southwest Border to enter the country.

Mr. PERRY. Thank you.

Thank you, Mr. Chairman.

Chairman MCCAUL. The Chairman now recognizes Ms. Clarke.

Ms. CLARKE. Thank you very much, Mr. Chairman.

I want to first of all, just applaud all of your efforts to keep the American people safe and secure. You know, I think all of my colleagues have stated it, but I wanted to emphasize that since 9/11, we have really progressed and stood up in infrastructure that has, for the most part, kept our Nation safe from foreign terrorist attacks.

I want to also wish you much continued success in all of your endeavors.

I want to drill down a little bit more on the subject of cybersecurity, particularly the workforce. We have heard a number of colleagues raise it today. But I know that the Federal, State, and law enforcement organizations face challenges in having the appropriate number of skilled investigators, forensic examiners, and prosecutors.

We all know that the pool of qualified candidates are limited, because individuals involved in investigating or examining cyber crime are highly trained specialists, requiring both law enforcement and technical skills.

According to some, once an investigator or an examiner specializes in cyber crime, it takes up to 12 months for that individual to really become proficient in the use of those skills. Add to that the competitive nature of the arena, the difficulty of competing with the private sector.

So, my question to you is: When we know that it is a challenge to recruit such individuals from a limited pool of available talent, retain them in the face of private sector competing offers, and train them up, to date, with changing technology and increasingly sophisticated criminal techniques, how are you dealing with this specialized manpower issue in your agencies?

I want to also submit to you that while today we are not necessarily seeing the nexus between advanced terrorist activity through the use of the internet, I can envision theft that then feeds money into these enterprises, and I am sure you can as well—as creative as we can be in our minds, they too can be creative.

So, would you just share with us some of your thoughts?

Secretary JOHNSON. I will start with that. I agree that talent, cyber talent is critical to our efforts.

I have personally engaged in recruitment efforts, and have encouraged young people in graduate schools in the cyber corridor in northern Louisiana, Georgia Tech, and other places, to consider a career or at least a short period of time before they go into the private sector working for DHS or the FBI or some other place, to serve their country.

There is a tremendous level of learning they can get by serving their country in the cybersecurity world, even for a short period of time.

But Congress can help us with this. There is a bill pending right now, I think on the Senate side, to enhance my cyber hiring capability, and I am hoping along with some other pending legislation in cyber that the Congress will act on that. Because I do need help in attracting cyber talent.

Ms. CLARKE. What about the issue of retention? Are you finding that people come—and I mean is it an ebb and a flow? How do we maintain——

Secretary JOHNSON. I just lost a very, very valued member of my cybersecurity team to Citigroup. So, yes, there is an issue with retention. Financial sector has much more capability to offer, very attractive packages, than either Jim or I do.

So, even though everybody knows it is cool working for the FBI——

Ms. CLARKE. Do either of you want to add to that?

Mr. COMEY. I don't want Secretary Johnson to know my secrets, because I am competing for the same talent. But he just figured one out. It is much cooler to work for the FBI.

[Laughter.]

Mr. COMEY. That is part of my pitch. But it is a big challenge.

Secretary JOHNSON. Everyone watching on C–SPAN, I was joking.

Mr. COMEY. I oversaw security in two major private-sector enterprises before returning to Government, so I used to compete from that side for talent. The amount of money that is paid to these young folks, doesn't have to be young, but folks with talent, we can't compete with.

So—but I believe we can compete on the nature of our mission.

All right, you are not going to make much of a living doing what we do, but what I say to young people is, "you are going to make a life that is unlike any other, because you are going to be saving lives." That is what we do for a living. So that is a different way to think about work, but I think it is a place we can and should compete for these folks.

Chairman MCCAUL. Chairman recognizes Mr. Sanford.

Mr. SANFORD. Thank you, Mr. Chairman.

Again, thanks to each one of you for coming, testifying before the committee.

You know, in as much as today's hearings about world-wide threats to the homeland and in as much as we are going to take a fairly significant vote today with regard to homeland threats, I would be curious to hear each one of your perspectives on what you view to be the biggest deficiency with regard to that plan that we will vote on today.

Secretary JOHNSON. I would say that the plan the President has put forward to deal with ISIL, assuming that is what you are referring to——

Mr. SANFORD. Yes, sir.

Secretary JOHNSON [continuing]. Is a strong plan in many respects. We have got to work with an international coalition, we have got to work to support the efforts made by the new Iraqi government, and we have got to take the fight directly to ISIL.

So, I think it is incumbent upon Congress to act on the authorities we have requested. I think the President himself has said that we cannot expect this—we cannot expect to deal with this threat overnight. It is going to take an enduring, sustained effort.

So, I hope Congress will support our efforts in that regard.

Mr. SANFORD. Well, might I interject there? I continue to always be impressed with your skills, as a former lawyer.

What I asked was for the biggest deficiency is.

Secretary JOHNSON. I would refer you to the State Department and the Defense Department, Congressman.

But I believe that our proposal and our plan is a strong one for degrading and ultimately defeating ISIL.

Mr. SANFORD. It is a pass, I understand. Anybody else want to take a crack at the apple?

Mr. COMEY. I just don't think that is something that, at the FBI I can or should comment on.

Mr. SANFORD. Okay.

Mr. OLSEN. I agree.

Mr. SANFORD. All right. I got three passes on that one. How many—let me rephrase the question then.

You know, von Clausewitz, in his study of war, talked about how is it that you impact your enemy's center of gravity? Many people have argued that what we are doing, though it is action, it is engagement, that it is doing something, we are not at the end of the day impacting the enemy's center of gravity and their ability to bring harm to the United States.

Are there any thoughts, if you were to pick one thing that you think would impact the terrorism threat to the United States these days or around the world, what do you think to be their primary weakness, that center of gravity that, if affected, would really begin to impact the outcomes?

Secretary JOHNSON. Congressman, let me answer that question this way.

From my DHS experience and from my Department of Defense experience, I think that it is important that in our efforts, we not enable the enemy to recruit faster than we can capture or kill the enemy. So, and particularly when it comes to the homeland.

So, along with the efforts of our military, and along with the efforts of our partners overseas to take the fight directly to ISIL, there has to be an effort at countering their propaganda, their social media. There has to be an effort at engaging potential violent extremist threats here at home, because, as has been pointed out by many Members of this committee, these groups in the current age are very good at propaganda, at recruitment without having to recruit somebody and indoctrinate them in a terrorist training camp.

So, I am focused on countering violent extremism at home. Together, we are focused on counteracting the literature and the propaganda, the notion that ISIL is an Islamic state, which is false. It is not a state, and it is not Islamic. It is a group of murderers and kidnappers who commit genocide. So, they are a group of depraved individuals who have captured the world's attention right now.

So, I think I am addressing the premise of your question, which is that it has got to be a comprehensive effort that involves multiple agencies of our Government.

Mr. SANFORD. I see I am down to 30 seconds, so let me just skip to my last question, very, very quickly.

That is, given what some of the testimony has uncovered with regard to this constantly recurring theme of roughly 6 percent operational control, based on GAO report with regard to the border, our Southern Border, why not, again, simply build a fence?

I would be curious to hear each one of your quick thoughts as to, yes or no, why not simply build a fence?

Secretary JOHNSON. Would you like me to start?

Mr. SANFORD. Well, you filibuster the best. So, I think I would rather go to the others first.

Mr. COMEY. I am just going to give you a pass so I can pitch it back to him.

Mr. OLSEN. Yes, really, pass as well, since it is not really within our remit.

Secretary JOHNSON. First of all, Congressman, what we do on the Southern Border depends in very large part on the resources that Congress is willing to give us, so——

Mr. SANFORD. So, absent the resource question, what would be your recommendation? Why not simply build a fence?

Secretary JOHNSON. My recommendation is the most effective, efficient use of our resources is a risk-based strategy. I do not believe that building a wall across the entire Southwest Border is an appropriate use of taxpayer dollars.

If I build a 15-foot wall, somebody is going to build a 16-foot ladder. So, we have the technology in place, and we need more to be able to look to where the risk——

Mr. SANFORD. I might interject, they might build a 16-foot wall, but it would certainly not allow school-age children to walk up to officers and hand themselves over.

Secretary JOHNSON. Very definitely, the situation we faced this summer was one where many of these kids wanted to get caught. So, when you are dealing with that kind of situation, it is important to demonstrate that our—that if you come here, you will be apprehended, and we will send you back.

So we stepped up our ability to send people back quicker. We engaged in a pretty aggressive public messaging campaign about the hazards of doing that. But again, when we go down that road, we need a partner in Congress. I didn't get one this summer.

I asked for money to help pay for our efforts to step up our border security, and we didn't get help. I now have to pay for it——

Mr. SANFORD. I have many, many different thoughts on that, but I see I have entirely burned through my time, Mr. Chairman. To be continued, sir.

Chairman MCCAUL. Thank you, sir.

The Chairman recognizes Mr. Richmond.

Mr. RICHMOND. Thank you, Mr. Chairman, and thank you to the witnesses here, who play a great part in protecting the area I represent in Louisiana. With that, let me just ask, because I heard it said before that cybersecurity and our home-grown terrorists are really what keeps us up at night. It was mentioned that especially with the home-grown terrorists, it is someone—well, cybersecurity could be someone sitting in their basement on a computer trying to wreak havoc.

So, we know what we do, Secretary Johnson, in terms of our chemical facilities and making sure that they are equipped to deal with those types of things. But in Louisiana we also have a number of ports and shipping companies. We have the loop that handles at its peak over 1.2 million barrels of oil a day and is responsible for probably 50 percent of oil getting to the refineries in Louisiana.

How confident are we that we are communicating enough with State police, local police, wildlife and fisheries, and all the other departments to make sure that our facilities offshore and our facilities that connect are covered?

Also embedded in that question is making sure that the intelligence sharing is there and that our State police and local police have done what they need to do to have the clearance.

Secretary JOHNSON. Going back to what Director Comey said, I would welcome the opportunity to be in a position to share more with our State and local partners in terms of Classified information once they have a security clearance and a background check. I think it is in all of our interest that we do that.

I have been impressed in the 9 months I have been in office with the level of cooperation and participation we get from State and local law enforcement. I think in some areas of the country the relationships are better than in others.

I have also visited a number of ports. I haven't been to—I have been to the Coast Guard station in New Orleans. I have not—I don't know that I have been to the commercial port there, but I have been to a number of ports. I have been impressed with our level of cooperation with local authorities.

But we have got to keep at it and we can always do a better job. Port security is one of my priorities while I am in office.

Mr. RICHMOND. The other thing—and you talked about resources especially in response to the question from my colleague Mr. Sanford. What other resources that—do you think that we could provide local governments to help them with homeland security? I know that with different port police departments you all have offered license plate scanners and they can apply for grants to do things of that nature.

But in a city like New Orleans, for example, that brings in about over 9 million visitors a year, hosts Super Bowls, National championships, Mardi Gras, all of those things, outside of just the area of the ports, assets like those could be very, very valuable.

The question becomes what do you think the role is of the Federal Government to assist local police departments and State police in getting that equipment that would make the country more safe, especially when you have events that have millions of people in town at a time?

Secretary JOHNSON. I think the principal means is our grant-making activity. Through our grants, we fund a number of different programs, training, the ability to provide equipment for homeland security. So I think grants is the principal means by which we should do that.

I want to make sure that we have our grant formulas correct. That is something I am looking into. I want to make sure that we—our grant making around the country is at appropriate levels.

Mr. RICHMOND. Mr. Comey, Mr. Olsen, I will just ask you slight request, and if you want to reply it would be great. To the extent that your intelligence sharing and your effectiveness also goes hand-in-hand with the ability and competence of local police departments, and you all do a great job what you do, but you can't be successful if the local police departments are not focused and competent in doing what they do.

To that extent, do you all have a mechanism to let Members of Congress know, hey, your police department is slacking in some areas that could make your communities unsafe? I think it is something that all the Members of Congress would take great interest in to make sure that they know all of the police departments and sheriffs in their area are focused on it.

If they are not, we may have to give them that extra push to get them there. So can you provide us that information and do you see cases of that?

Mr. COMEY. It is a good question, Congressman. I don't know is the answer. I don't think there is a vehicle for us to do that. In a way, we don't focus a lot on that because if we see a problem we try and work with that partner to help them fix that problem. If they need resources, we go to Jeh's people, see if a grant can be made. So the answer is I don't think so.

Mr. OLSEN. I agree with Director Comey on that point. I am not sure that I have seen an actual mechanism. Obviously we—as Director Comey said, we just try to fix those problems when we see them in the field.

It is something that from my vantage point, NCTC, we work through DHS and FBI in any outreach we have with State and local law enforcement. But I do agree with your fundamental point that it is fundamentally our best line of defense, our first line of defense against any sort of particularly home-grown attack.

Mr. RICHMOND. Well thank you for your questions. I would just say that if you see that any of my law enforcement chiefs, if they don't get it, please let me know that they don't get it so that I can get involved.

Thank you, Mr. Chairman. Again, thank you for calling this meeting.

Chairman MCCAUL. Thank you.

Let me thank the witnesses for being here today. I think it has been an excellent discussion. Great oversight hearing.

Mr. Secretary, as always, thank you for being here and thanks for your outreach to this committee.

Matt, we wish you well in your future endeavors, and I know we will be talking about that personally.

Director Comey, I think it speaks volumes, your presence here today, of a new era being ushered in with the FBI and DHS and State and locals coordinating and working together, which I always think is the best formula which actually does sort-of epitomize what the JTTFs were founded to do in the first place. But I think your leadership and being here today, I just can't tell you how much I appreciate it.

So with that, Members may have additional questions in writing. With that, this hearing stands adjourned.

[Whereupon, at 12:31 p.m., the committee was adjourned.]

APPENDIX

QUESTIONS FROM HONORABLE PAUL C. BROUN FOR JEH C. JOHNSON

Question 1a. Do we know how many Americans have attempted to join the Islamic State of Iraq and the Levant (ISIL) and other similar terrorist organizations?

How many have succeeded?

Answer. Recent estimates indicate there are as many as 16,000 foreign fighters, of which 2,700 or so are Westerners. DHS is aware of over 100 U.S. persons who have traveled to Syria or sought to travel to Syria to join terrorist groups operating there, including the Islamic State of Iraq and the Levant (ISIL), al-Nusrah Front, and other violent terrorist groups. We can provide a more comprehensive answer, including details on how many have succeeded, in a Classified setting[1] (see Classified appendix).

Question 1b. Our current policy is not to suspend the passports of American citizens who we believe are traveling overseas with the intention of joining organizations dedicated to doing harm to America and American interests. Why should these individuals be allowed to continue traveling on an American passport? Is it time to reconsider and reevaluate this policy?

Answer. DHS works with its interagency partners, including the Department of Justice, the Federal Bureau of Investigation, and the State Department to identify and act on cases where individual's activities abroad could cause serious damage to the National security or foreign policy of the United States. In certain circumstances, the Department of State has the authority to revoke or limit passports on a case-by-case basis, which can be expedited when the situation warrants. Working with interagency partners, DHS retains a range of tools to identify and disrupt threats from terrorist travel.

Question 1c. Does the Department of Homeland Security communicate with the Department of State to request that these individuals' passports be suspended or revoked? If not, why?

Answer. DHS works with our interagency law enforcement, intelligence, and military partners, including the Department of State, to identify actual and potential U.S. citizen foreign terrorist fighters, and will, if and when appropriate, recommend that the Department of State use its authorities to revoke the U.S. passports of these individuals.

Question 2. Of these individuals who have traveled overseas with the aim of joining terrorist organizations, have any of them attempted to return to the United States? How many?

How are the Department of Homeland Security and the Federal Bureau of Investigation monitoring these individuals upon their return to the United States?

Answer. We have seen a few instances where U.S. persons who traveled to Syria to join terrorist groups have returned to the United States. We can provide more details in a Classified setting (see Classified appendix).

As with any terrorism investigation, DHS provides appropriate support to the Federal Bureau of Investigation (FBI) through Joint Terrorism Task Forces that manage the investigations. We respectfully defer to the FBI on the details of how their investigative subjects are monitored.

Question 3. Several American cities and even the State of California have declared themselves to be "sanctuaries" that will protect individuals who have illegally immigrated into the United States. Although there are certainly many illegal immigrants who are not terrorists or potential terrorists, I am concerned about the prospect of dangerous individuals also seeking shelter in these communities where they know that they will not be questioned about their identity or immigrant status. Do you believe that the potential of dangerous individuals who may have ties to terrorist

---

[1] From Testimony of NCTC Director Matthew Olsen at hearing on *Worldwide Threats to the Homeland* (September 17, 2014).

organizations hiding amongst these "sanctuaries" is a threat to our National security?

Answer. DHS is concerned about any methods used by terrorists to gain access to the United States. We can provide more details about our assessment in a Classified setting (see Classified appendix).

Question 4a. I believe that our failure to completely secure the border is a threat to our National security. Individuals can enter our Nation illegally without being intercepted by border law enforcement. How can the Department of Homeland Security know the number of people and from where they originate if they are not first intercepted at the border?

If there are unknown individuals crossing the border into the United States, how can we be sure that none of these individuals are members or have ties to terrorist organizations?

Question 4b. If we cannot be sure of the identities of individuals entering our country illegally, then how can we be sure that these individuals are not bringing dangerous materials and weapons into the country to be used against our citizens?

Answer. DHS is committed to prioritizing and focusing our efforts to best protect the American public from threats such as terrorism, illegal drug and precursor trafficking, human trafficking and illegal migration, and arms traffic, while simultaneously facilitating and securing lawful flows of people, goods, and intellectual property through all potential transit pathways.

We are continually refining our risk-based strategy and layered approach to border security, extending our borders outward, and focusing our resources on the greatest risks to interdict threats before they reach the United States. The success of our targeted security measures depends in great part on our ability to gather, analyze, share, and respond to information in a timely manner—using predictive intelligence and analysis to identify existing and emerging threat streams to target responses. Our success also depends in part on our U.S. Border Patrol's mobile and dynamic workforce, in order to assign agents to address evolving threats.

Question 5a. What specific threats does the Islamic State of Iraq and the Levant (ISIL) pose to our homeland?

What centers of American interests overseas are threatened by ISIL?

Answer. To date we have no information suggesting that the ISIL is currently plotting attacks against the United States. However, an ISIL spokesman on September 21, 2014, issued a statement calling for attacks on all countries involved in the coalition targeting the group in Iraq and Syria, including the United States and France. This is the first time we have seen the group's leadership explicitly calling for attacks on the United States; their previous messaging had called on individuals, including Westerners, to travel to Iraq and Syria to join the group's efforts there.

We remain concerned that individuals inspired by the group, including some in the United States, could seek to follow the group's advice and carry out attacks here, although to date we have no information suggesting U.S.-based ISIL adherents are plotting attacks inside the United States. As the arrest of an individual seeking to travel to Iraq or Syria at Chicago-O'Hare International Airport in early October indicates, group sympathizers will likely primarily remain focused on traveling to Syria or Iraq for the time being.

We do assess that ISIL poses a more significant direct threat to U.S. interests in Iraq, Syria, and the immediate region. We respectfully defer to the FBI and the Department of State on this issue, however.

Question 5b. What specific threats does the Islamic State of Iraq and the Levant (ISIL) pose to our homeland?

Do you believe that this threat justifies a declaration of war against ISIL?

Answer. DHS takes no position on whether the threat posed by ISIL justifies a declaration of war.

Question 6. I am a firm believer in the importance of human intelligence in our National security strategy. Do we currently have enough human intelligence capacity—both here in the homeland and overseas—to counter the threats posed by state and non-state actors alike?

Answer. DHS is working on increasing its human intelligence-gathering capabilities at home and anticipates increasing its field collector/reporter personnel by 50 percent, from 19 to approximately 30, during the coming year. We are also training Intelligence Officers in State and major urban area fusion centers to do intelligence reporting. This will increase the human intelligence capability by additional 50–60 personnel.

The DHS Intelligence Enterprise has increased intelligence reporting, producing over 3,000 reports in fiscal year 2014.

An assessment of homeland intelligence capability would require consideration of the FBI role and input from the Office of the Director of National Intelligence (ODNI).

Assessment of the overseas capability is outside of the DHS mission and should be directed to the ODNI.

QUESTIONS FROM HONORABLE RON BARBER FOR JEH C. JOHNSON

Question 1. What is the Department of Homeland Security doing to prevent so-called "lone-wolf" acts of terror and how are you engaging local communities in these efforts?

Answer. The Department remains concerned about the consistent level of home-grown violent extremism (HVE) activity, as well as the potential for conflict areas such as Syria to inspire and mobilize U.S.- and Europe-based home-grown violent extremists to participate in or support acts of violence.

We understand that the threat posed by violent extremism is neither constrained by international borders nor limited to any single ideology. Groups and individuals inspired by a range of religious, political, or other ideological beliefs have promoted and used violence against the United States.

Moreover, increasingly sophisticated use of the internet, mainstream and social media, and information technology by violent extremists add an additional layer of complexity.

To counter violent extremism (CVE), the Department is working with a broad range of partners to gain a better understanding of the behaviors, tactics, and other indicators that could point to potential terrorist activity within the United States or against U.S. interests abroad, and the best ways to mitigate or prevent that activity.

COMMUNITY ENGAGEMENT

To counter violent extremism, the Department regularly engages with diverse community groups across the United States in order to strengthen resiliency to violent extremist recruitment efforts. Using existing community engagement efforts, as well as participatory trust-building processes, these efforts aim to empower community opposition to violent extremism. Active engagement with diverse communities can undermine key recruiting narratives used by violent extremist groups, such as al-Qaeda, al-Nusrah Front, and Islamic State of Iraq and the Levant (ISIL).

Accordingly, the Department has implemented a number of community engagement efforts as part of its broader CVE mandate. These include:

- *Community Awareness Briefing (CAB).*—DHS's Office for Civil Rights and Civil Liberties (CRCL) and the National Counterterrorism Center's (NCTC) Directorate of Strategic Operational Planning (DSOP) developed and implemented the Community Awareness Briefing, designed to share Unclassified information with communities regarding the threat of violent extremism.
- *Community Resiliency Exercise (CREX).*—The CREX was developed by DHS CRCL and NCTC's DSOP to increase trust between communities and law enforcement officials. The CREX is a half-day table-top exercise designed to improve communication between law enforcement and communities and to share ideas on how best to build community resilience against violent extremism.
- CRCL has held more than 100 community engagement events over the past few years, and more than 5,000 State and Local Law Enforcement and fusion center personnel have been trained by CRCL on cultural awareness and how to best engage with communities at over 75 training events and National law enforcement conferences.
- CRCL has led an enhanced engagement initiative around the country with key leaders and officials of Syrian-American organizations who have become strong partners.

Question 2. As we work to defeat ISIL, what steps can we also take in our National counterterrorism strategy to ensure another group does not take ISIL's place?

Answer. Current U.S. strategy is working to degrade, dismantle, and ultimately defeat ISIL. This strategy includes lines of effort to support effective governance in Iraq, to deny terrorist groups a safe haven in Iraq and Syria, and to promote an eventual peaceful settlement of the conflict in Syria. U.S. counterterrorism strategy includes measures to protect the American people, the U.S. homeland, and American interests, both at home and abroad. It involves military, intelligence, security, diplomatic, and law enforcement efforts to disrupt, degrade, dismantle, and defeat al-Qaeda and its affiliates and adherents. It includes efforts to prevent terrorists from developing, acquiring, and using weapons of mass destruction. It also includes efforts to eliminate terrorist safe havens, build enduring counterterrorism partnerships and capabilities, and counter al-Qaeda's ideology and violent extremism generally. Efforts are underway to deny ISIL, al-Qaeda, and other terrorist groups the access to resources and financial networks.

As noted in the National Counterterrorism Strategy, there are steps that the United States can take, and is taking, to address the causes that motivate terrorism and violent extremism, and to take additional measures to protect our security when a group poses a threat to U.S. National security interests. It is important that those contemplating whether to engage in terrorist acts see a united opposition against them, not just from the United States, but from other nations and societies as well.

In addition to addressing terrorist threats directly when they arise, the United States holds core values of respect for human rights; encouraging responsive governance; respect for privacy rights, civil liberties, and civil rights; balancing security and transparency; and upholding the rule of law. As our National Counterterrorism Strategy says, the power and appeal of our values enables the United States to build a broad coalition to act collectively against the common threat posed by terrorists, further delegitimizing, isolating, and weakening our adversaries.

Question 3. How are you currently collaborating with local law enforcement to protect "soft targets" in our communities and what potential gaps in education or training remain?

Answer. DHS, alongside Federal and State, local, Tribal, and territorial, and private-sector partners, identifies and assesses a myriad of potential and actual threats to the United States. It is critical that all partners work together to effectively prevent and protect against these varying and complex threats.

Collectively, DHS and intelligence community partners, to include the FBI, draft and disseminate joint intelligence products to State, local, Tribal, and territorial customers. For threat indicators originating at the local level, DHS works in concert with State, local, Tribal, and territorial partners to provide DHS information and intelligence holdings necessary to accurately identify and characterize threats.

A key aspect in developing, maintaining, and exercising these threat-related mission contributions with State, local, Tribal, and territorial partners are Nationally-deployed DHS Intelligence Officers. Intelligence Officers aid and support State, local, Tribal, and territorial partners by supporting the access, analysis, and dissemination of DHS and Federal intelligence products, specifically how these National-level products impact States and localities.

Assisting State, local, Tribal, and territorial partners in threat mitigation and application of protective measures, Intelligence Officers work closely with DHS's Protective Security Advisors. Protective Security Advisors are critical partners and assist in conducting vulnerability assessments, serving as critical infrastructure liaisons, and security planning. Protective Security Advisors' capabilities and contributions can be applied to "hard" and "soft" targets. This spans from chemical manufacturing sites and transportation nodes, to mass gathering special events, large retail locations, and other "soft target" sites.

With respect to training and education, the State, local, Tribal, and territorial community is complex and diverse in terms of protection capabilities. DHS's close partnership with State, local, Tribal, and territorial partners provides a means to not only share and understand threats but also work to offer technical capabilities, training, and educational assistance based on needs.

QUESTION FROM HONORABLE DONALD M. PAYNE FOR JEH C. JOHNSON

Question. Thank you for your testimony, and for what you do to ensure that appropriate steps are taken to continue protecting our homeland. During the hearing, you made it clear that DHS has the Student and Exchange Visitor Information System (SEVIS) in place to track and monitor foreign students. The SEVIS database called into question whether some students were in compliance with their immigration status. It is my understanding that the immigration status of these foreign students may have been unclear because they changed their school enrollment status, received a green card, or obtained an H1B visa. While testifying, you agreed with this assessment, but also stated that some of these students have been arrested for noncompliance. Can you please clarify your testimony by distinguishing between arrests for terrorist-related offenses, if any, and non-terrorism issues?

Answer. Of the potential visa overstay candidates you reference in your question who may possibly be the subject of criminal investigation by U.S. Immigration and Customs Enforcement's Office of Homeland Security Investigations, we can clarify that none of these individuals are currently being investigated for any terrorism-related offenses.

QUESTIONS FROM HONORABLE PAUL C. BROUN FOR JAMES B. COMEY

Question 1a. Do we know how many Americans have attempted to join the Islamic State of Iraq and the Levant (ISIL) and other similar terrorist organizations? How many have succeeded?

Question 1b. Our current policy is not to suspend the passports of American citizens who we believe are traveling overseas with the intention of joining organizations dedicated to doing harm to America and American interests. Why should these individuals be allowed to continue traveling on an American passport? Is it time to reconsider and reevaluate this policy?

Question 1c. Does the Department of Homeland Security communicate with the Department of State to request that these individuals' passports be suspended or revoked? If not, why?

Answer. Response was not received at the time of publication.

Question 2. Of these individuals who have traveled overseas with the aim of joining terrorist organizations, have any of them attempted to return to the United States? How many?

How are the Department of Homeland Security and the Federal Bureau of Investigation monitoring these individuals upon their return to the United States?

Answer. Response was not received at the time of publication.

Question 3. Several American cities and even the State of California have declared themselves to be "sanctuaries" that will protect individuals who have illegally immigrated into the United States. Although there are certainly many illegal immigrants who are not terrorists or potential terrorists, I am concerned about the prospect of dangerous individuals also seeking shelter in these communities where they know that they will not be questioned about their identity or immigrant status. Do you believe that the potential of dangerous individuals who may have ties to terrorist organizations hiding amongst these "sanctuaries" is a threat to our National security?

Answer. Response was not received at the time of publication.

Question 4a. I believe that our failure to completely secure the border is a threat to our National security. Individuals can enter our Nation illegally without being intercepted by border law enforcement. How can the Department of Homeland Security know the number of people and from where they originate if they are not first intercepted at the border?

If there are unknown individuals crossing the border into the United States, how can we be sure that none of these individuals are members or have ties to terrorist organizations?

Question 4b. If we cannot be sure of the identities of individuals entering our country illegally, then how can we be sure that these individuals are not bringing dangerous materials and weapons into the country to be used against our citizens?

Answer. Response was not received at the time of publication.

Question 5a. What specific threats does the Islamic State of Iraq and the Levant (ISIL) pose to our homeland?

What centers of American interests overseas are threatened by ISIL?

Question 5b. Do you believe that this threat justifies a declaration of war against ISIL?

Answer. Response was not received at the time of publication.

Question 6. I am a firm believer in the importance of human intelligence in our National security strategy. Do we currently have enough human intelligence capacity—both here in the homeland and overseas—to counter the threats posed by state and non-state actors alike?

Answer. Response was not received at the time of publication.

QUESTIONS FROM HONORABLE PAUL C. BROUN FOR MATTHEW G. OLSEN

Question 1a. Do we know how many Americans have attempted to join the Islamic State of Iraq and the Levant (ISIL) and other similar terrorist organizations? How many have succeeded?

Question 1b. Our current policy is not to suspend the passports of American citizens who we believe are traveling overseas with the intention of joining organizations dedicated to doing harm to America and American interests. Why should these individuals be allowed to continue traveling on an American passport? Is it time to reconsider and reevaluate this policy?

Question 1c. Does the Department of Homeland Security communicate with the Department of State to request that these individuals' passports be suspended or revoked? If not, why?

Answer. Response was not received at the time of publication.

Question 2. Of these individuals who have traveled overseas with the aim of joining terrorist organizations, have any of them attempted to return to the United States? How many?

How are the Department of Homeland Security and the Federal Bureau of Investigation monitoring these individuals upon their return to the United States?

Answer. Response was not received at the time of publication.

Question 3. Several American cities and even the State of California have declared themselves to be "sanctuaries" that will protect individuals who have illegally immigrated into the United States. Although there are certainly many illegal immigrants who are not terrorists or potential terrorists, I am concerned about the prospect of dangerous individuals also seeking shelter in these communities where they know that they will not be questioned about their identity or immigrant status. Do you believe that the potential of dangerous individuals who may have ties to terrorist organizations hiding amongst these "sanctuaries" is a threat to our National security?

Answer. Response was not received at the time of publication.

Question 4a. I believe that our failure to completely secure the border is a threat to our National security. Individuals can enter our Nation illegally without being intercepted by border law enforcement. How can the Department of Homeland Security know the number of people and from where they originate if they are not first intercepted at the border?

If there are unknown individuals crossing the border into the United States, how can we be sure that none of these individuals are members or have ties to terrorist organizations?

Question 4b. If we cannot be sure of the identities of individuals entering our country illegally, then how can we be sure that these individuals are not bringing dangerous materials and weapons into the country to be used against our citizens?

Answer. Response was not received at the time of publication.

Question 5a. What specific threats does the Islamic State of Iraq and the Levant (ISIL) pose to our homeland?

What centers of American interests overseas are threatened by ISIL?

Question 5b. Do you believe that this threat justifies a declaration of war against ISIL?

Answer. Response was not received at the time of publication.

Question 6. I am a firm believer in the importance of human intelligence in our National security strategy. Do we currently have enough human intelligence capacity—both here in the Homeland and overseas—to counter the threats posed by state and non-state actors alike?

Answer. Response was not received at the time of publication.

QUESTION FROM HONORABLE SUSAN W. BROOKS FOR MATTHEW G. OLSEN

Question. There have been recent media reports of a laptop seized from a building occupied by ISIS containing files describing methods to grow and disseminate biological pathogens. These reports, if true, indicate an interest on the part of ISIS to develop and deploy biological weapons. ISIS may also have the opportunity to develop such weapons, having access to university laboratories in Iraq. Considering this interest and opportunity, while acknowledging that there are significant technical hurdles that must be overcome to develop such weapons, I am interested in your assessment of ISIS' capability to develop and deploy biological weapons.

Answer. Response was not received at the time of publication.

○